THEY ALL SANG ON THE CORNER

New York City's Rhythm and Blues Vocal Groups of the 1950's

PHILIP GROIA

THEY ALL SANG ON THE CORNER

New York City's Rhythm and Blues Vocal Groups of the 1950's

Philip Groia

The Edmond Publishing Company

Setauket, New York, 11733

All We Have To Keep Us Is Our Memories Of You

Cover,Photo,and Art Direction by Nick Schillizzi

FOREWORD

The author is indebted to many people who have contributed precious time and knowledge. A list of acknowledgments appears at the end of the book. Special thanks must go to Mrs. Marcia Vance who typed the original manuscript. Disc jockeys, Tom Luciani and Joe Marchesani of The Time Capsule Show (WFUV-FM in New York City) deserve credit for keeping the interest alive in those vocal groups who sang Rhythm and Blues and Rock'n' Roll music of the 1950's. They were radio pioneers in giving information about black groups back in 1963 when playing old records was not considered fashionable. Many leads and personal anecdotes could not have been obtained without the friendly cooperation of two other disc jockeys, Al Grannum (KAGB-FM in Inglewood, California) and Bobby Jay (WWRL-AM in New York City).

But especially to those who sang on the corner and have succeeded at their chosen art, thank you. To those who have not fared as well, They All Sang On The Corner is dedicated to you.

CONTENTS

Preface

The current tide of literature dealing with the nostalgia of the 1950's decade and more specifically with the roots of contemporary Rock music fails somewhat in accurately chronicling the importance of black Rhythm and Blues quartets and quintets. This book records the history of these groups and recognizes street corner singing as a musical and cultural medium.

The underlying assumption is that street corner singing in black neighborhoods, a cornerstone in R&B music, is a fundamental root in today's contemporary popular music. They All Sang On The Corner is a geographical, chronological and sociological study of R&B group singing. It is biographical, it is historically documented, and in parts is fictionalized to add excitement and color where recreation and source material is unavailable. It deals with the dynamics of the street corner and the art of four and five part harmony as outward manifestations of the interpersonal relationships of a specific neighborhood. Acappella street singing and the recording of it with accompaniment are dealt with as a social phenomenon of city life. Personal and group triumphs and tragedies are also included.

The book is limited to the study of male black groups who sang R&B music primarily on the streets of New York City during the period of 1947 through approximately 1960. This time limitation is, however, extended to cover those acts performing during the current wave of "Rock 'n' Roll Revival" shows. Female groups have been generally omitted for the purpose of brevity and that they were not that prevalent in the 1950's. However, where pertinent, some female singers have been included.

The overwhelming source of primary material is from personal interviews conducted with some or all of the original members of groups of the fifties. Disc jockeys, theatre owners, and record company executives have also been consulted. Secondary sources of information include the two journals of the popular music field: Billboard and Cash Box. Technical magazines dealing with the subject of R&B group harmony are also available: R&B Magazine, Record Exchanger, Big Town Review and Bim Bam Boom. The author is a contributor to Bim Bam Boom and Rock Review. Other information comes from a vast personal record collection, and a personal listening experience that dates back to 1954. Photographs of groups in studio or on-stage action poses are extensively used in the book. Many of these are previously unpublished.

Related Literature - There have been some books published dealing with the general subject of R&B music:

Garland, Phyll The Sound Of Soul,
       Henry Regnery,1969.

Gillett, Charlie The Sound Of The City,
       Outerbridge & Dienstfrey,1969.

McCutcheon, Lynn Rhythm And Blues,
       R.W.Beatty.Ltd.,1971.

Millar, Bill The Drifters,
       MacMillan,1972

Shaw, Arnold The World Of Soul,
       MacMillan,1969.

Although The Drifters has dealt with the personal and biographical history of one group, none of the above has chronicled the social dynamics of street corner singing, the influences of and contributions by the R&B groups of the fifties and the feelings of achievement and failure experienced by many of these performers.

Chapter I

Halloween 1954

On Halloween night the prospects for a thirteen year old Long Island City boy of ringing door bells, throwing eggs, making prank phone calls and raising Cain in the corner candy store affectionately called "Happy Harry's Fire House", seemed totally unexciting that October schoolnight in 1954. Being raised on a steady diet of Brahms and Beethoven offered not the slightest relief from the following morning's school day blues of attending that first period music appreciation class that held in store such choral delights as "It Will Take More Than A Pack Of Wild Horses" and "Oh, My Darlin' Clementine". As knowledge of the day's popular songs became increasingly acceptable with the gang in home-room 9-1, the search for radio station WINS at 8:30 P.M. took on new meaning as my AM radio dial was tuned that night.

Instead of finding "Sh-Boom" and "Please, Mr. Sandman", the songs white classmates had craved while dancing to the jukebox in the school cafeteria, one could hear a lusty, gravelly, barker type voice that introduced records as if they were tickets being hawked at a small town carnival sideshow; i.e.-Here's Buddy Milton with "Ooh Wahh!". Listening intently to that lonely radio station that night, weird, exotic, haunting and addictive medleys of "shoo-do-be-doo's", "ooh-bi-dee, ooh-bi-dee-ooh's", and "do-wop-shoo-bop-do-bah's" were heard. Listening to the conclusion of the program at 9:00 P.M., waiting fruitlessly for The Crew Cuts, Perry Como and the refugees from The Arthur Godfrey Show, The Chordettes, it soon became apparent that they would never be heard; not on Halloween, nor Thanksgiving nor any time on that program.

I had been introduced to Shirley Gunther and The Queens, The Harptones, The Moonglows and Moonlighters, Pee Wee Crayton, Danny Overbea and Lavern Baker. This was not "Listen To Lacy" but "Alan Freed's Rock 'n' Roll Party". I was hooked! Hooked on honking horns, rocking piano sets and electrical sounds accompanying male falsetto vocalists who sounded like nothing I had ever heard before, women whose vocalizing was equally astounding, lyrics I didn't understand and bass singers who confused everything with their "bop-bop-bye-oh's" and "doe-doe-doe-doe's". This was my music, something new

9

and refreshing, that I had discovered, cherished and worshipped all by myself. It wasn't until weeks later in the
school yard of Junior High School 126 that I learned that
there were others, as well, who appreciated and claimed for
their very own the piano staccato of Fats Domino's "I'm
Thinking Of You", The Three Chuckles' plaintive "Runaround"
and The Rivileers' haunting rendition of "I Love You For
Sentimental Reasons". As more and more schoolmates expressed
the same sentiments and selfish claims to those infectious
tunes and the provocative ringing and thumping of Alan
Freed's cow-bell and telephone book, I became more convinced
that I had truly discovered this thing called "Rock 'n'
Roll". Night after night I discovered over and over, The
Jewels, Nappy Brown, "Sax Man" Brown, Tommy Ridgely, The
Charms, The Clovers, Charlie and Ray, and all those vocal
groups who were named after cars, birds, animals and flowers
and whose tenor lead voices were so baffling.

Every day was a new discovery as the search continued
to find other stations with similar programs to meet the
needs of my new found musical tastes. One afternoon after
school, the search was rewarded at the end of the AM dial
by a resonant voiced disc jockey who played even more obscure melodies than Freed, called it "Rhythm and Blues"
instead of "Rock 'n' Roll" and who used a poetic "hype" with
his intro's: "Sit back, relax and enjoy the wax-from three-
oh-five, to five-three-oh--it's the Dr. Jive show!... Dr.
Jive? Tommy Smalls? Who were these guys?... As I listened
to The Casanovas, Buddy and Ella Johnson, Buddy and Claudia
and The Opals, my questions were answered as Tommy Smalls
was indeed Dr. Jive!

While privately digging The Moonglows, sport shirts with
the collars worn up and over black turtle necks, 1955 Olds
88's, and pegged pants; my "sissy" classmates, as one believed in undying adolescent certainty, were into white
button-down shirts, "d-a"-less haircuts, the Franco-Prus-
sian War, perpendicular lines in geometry, and pluperfect
tenses. But then the meeting of the minds occurred! One
afternoon when our French teacher asked us to reply in French
to the question "What is your favorite song?", Franco-Prus-
sian Steve answered, "Earth Angel" and button down Barry
offered "Shtiggy Boom". Wow! These guys with the big vocab-
ularies who read The New York Times and got 99's on algebra
tests had listened to Freed and Smalls too! I was now sure

10

that their mothers were also horrified at just the thought
of Joe Houston's tenor saxophone blaring through the house
on "Shtiggy Boom" accompanied by Freed's cow-bells and telephone directory.A visit to Steve's house confirmed this!
Pictures of Fats Domino and The Barons, lists of favorite
songs, 78 rpm records with Imperial and Atlantic labels
filled his room.
     Eventually in 1955 my family moved away from Long Island
City to the "clean air, low taxes" panacea of the suburbs.
Accompanying this odyssey to the suburbs were WINS, WLIB,
WNJR,and WWRL,a personal hatred for cover records that were
flooding the air waves at that time,and a devotion to black
street corner harmony;a loyalty and love that was still in
its infant stages. Perhaps this is how the obsession with
vocal group harmony began as I was so captivated by all those
background sounds which were in turn lead by the unique
voices of The Penguins' Cleve Duncan, or The Rivileers'
Gene Pearson,or The Robins' Grady Chapman.If you had been
exposed heretofore, to nothing but Caruso, Robert Merrill
and Guisseppe Di Stefano,then when you first heard The Solitaires and Bobby Williams plead "I Don't Stand A Ghost Of
A Chance", you too would have thought curiously about the
lead singer.And of course,never did I ever give the slightest thought that these singers, not being much older than
I, were black, and hailed from the ghettos of Harlem, Los
Angeles, Cincinnati, Chicago, and Cleveland.
     If I had to choose the one day when I became the totally
committed afficionado of the group sound,then it definitely
began on a cold,gray morning during the Christmas vacation
of 1955.Three of us, arose at dawn,trekked into Manhattan
to The Academy of Music Theatre on Fourteenth Street where
Alan Freed was presenting a Christmas revue including God
knows how many acts.Amidst all that screaming,screeching,
pushing,shoving,and language that my mother had spent fourteen years making sure I'd never use, I was treated to a
spectacle that is as vivid in memory today as it was in 1955.
After that huge orchestra of Freed's including Al Sears and
Sam "The Man" Taylor had blasted the roof off the place,
Freed introduced a group about which most of us knew very
little.Running on stage at full tilt came Bobby Mansfield
and The Wrens.Decked out conservatively in brown ivy league
suits,the group crouched behind Bobby as he crooned sugarly;

11

"ohh-ohh,well,come back my love" and in pursuit with arms waving in perfect unison, the group went down on one knee for all of us to hear;"wah-wah-wah-wah";then a quick step, a false move to the right,a shift to the left,and the bass singer bellowed into the mike;"I need your love so badly". What a sight!Harmony matched with different choreographic movements.On one number the sound system went dead and the group continued in perfect unison just as if nothing had happened.The Wrens were typical of the professionally polished who sold so few records that those made available are worth hundreds today with the artists receiving nothing.

A second spectacle of together singing was another of George Goldner's Rama groups,The Valentines,who were riding high on the crest of their second release,the New York street song called "Lily Maebelle".This time two microphones were used;one for tenor lead Richard Barrett and bass Ron Bright and the other for Eddie Edghill,Mickey Francis and Ray "Pops" Briggs. This was the first time I had ever seen five-part harmony demonstrated live with the bass singer alternating back and forth between his solo of "boh-boh-boh-boh-boh" on one mike and his harmonizing on the other as the group skipped and slided through that happy jump tune about somebody's little girl friend.This technique was demonstrated with even greater flair by The Heartbeats, who drew ooh's and ahh's and delirious shrieks as they did "Just A-Rockin' and A-Rollin' and A-Rhythm and A-Blues-in'" followed by the very popular grind "Crazy For You".White suits,red shirts with the "Mister-B" collars (worn up of course),white ties and white shoes all seemed to glowingly mesmerize our adolescent heads.James "Shep" Sheppard crooned and bass Wally Roker riffed together while Robby Brown, Albert Crump and Vernon Seavers looked as if they were walking in place as they accompanied with "dow-wah-wah-wah-wah"!

Closing out the program had to be the greatest stage performance ever presented in the history of Rhythm and Blues with the possible exceptions of The Temptations and James Brown. If you remember "No Chance", "Down The Road", and "Speedoo",then you listened to Earl Carroll,Earl Wade,Bobby Phillips, "Buddy" Brooks and Laverne Drake. The flashiest of all groups, they had chosen the right name in The Cadillacs.Every note, every bass riff,every vocal channel had been synchronized with corresponding choreography. Those white jackets,black trousers and those white shoes were a sight to behold as the group juked and bounced along as "Speedo",whose real name was Earl Carroll did his thing with straw hat and walking stick.The frenzy of the crowd would increase when little Bobby would join his "brother" Earl at one mike and do his "bom-bom-bom" or "I wonder why.....". Even the final fade out was staged so brilliantly that you just couldn't let the group leave as they disappeared,one by one, behind the curtain.

When we left the theatre that day it was as if we had just taken a shot of adrenalin. The feeling that pervaded everyone was one of identification;we just all had to have a singing group. The excitement swelled our heads so much that we boarded the BMT and headed,not for home;but to Flatbush and DeKalb Avenues in Brooklyn where Tommy Smalls had his own show at the Brooklyn Paramount.

When we walked into that huge auditorium the contrast was astounding.The predominantly black audience,much older than Freed's adolescent followers, had barely half-filled the theatre. In retrospect this was the first evidence for me that this music belonged to the black people of the great cities of America;a music that expressed frustration,happiness,sadness and just plain good talk about girlfriends and getting high. On stage were some of the greatest performers in R&B.As we walked in, Mickey "Guitar" Baker and Willis "Gator Tail" Jackson were accompanying Ruth Brown on "Mama,He Treats Your Daughter Mean".Also present were Clyde McPhatter who had just left The Drifters, Bo Diddley, The Five Keys, The Four Fellows, The Turbans,whose heads were appropriately adorned and the finest of all from Chicago, The Flamingos. Having witnessed The Cadillacs previously, had a sobering effect when Johnny Carter sang "That's My Baby" as he was "boom-chick-a-boomed" from that other mike by the Carey cousins, Paul Wilson and Nate Nelson. Somersaults and splits excited everybody but I especially remember the extending and retracting of the arms in "I-I-I-I-I-Want To Love You".But nothing could match that velvet blend of voices echoing throughout that famous house of Rock 'n' Roll as the "voice of champagne",Nate Nelson,sang "I'll Be Home".

To chronicle the advent,growth,development and influence on other musical forms of street corner Rhythm and Blues singing groups,from their inception in the 1940's through their relative demise in the early 1960's and revival in 1969, is to say the least an unwieldy task. It may be approached from the early influence of The Mills Brothers and The Ink Spots to the pioneer spirit of The Ravens,Orioles, Clovers,Drifters,Five Keys,Swallows, Larks and Moonglows. Or it can be traced geographically; i.e.Chicago-The Flamingos,

Cleveland-The Moonglows,Los Angeles -The Penguins,New Haven-The Nutmegs,and Five Satins,New York-The Harptones and Baltimore- The Orioles and Swallows.Or yet it can be followed by group nomenclature by which groups were named after birds, cars, lovers,animals, musical terms,age groups,cosmetics, card games and flowers,as witnessed by The Crows,Cadillacs, Heartbeats and Lovenotes,Spaniels,Cleftones and Channels, Teenagers, Avons,Solitaires and Jacks, and The Marigolds. Or perhaps it might be a good idea to forego all of these methods and just tell about those good old singing groups, many of which came from the streets of New York City.

Chapter 2

How It All Began

Rhythm and Blues vocal groups that appeared at those mid 1950's stage shows had to have been influenced by some earlier forms of music. It is safe to assume that this phenomenon of the Rhythm and Blues vocal group had its musical roots based in an earlier form of the black cultural idiom. "Rhythm and Blues" and "Rock and Roll", two terms long associated with the street corner vocal group, had their origins in another label or term for black music. This earlier form of popular black music was sung by blacks especially for blacks, played on black oriented stations and recorded by white managed recording companies whose product was sold in predominantly black neighborhoods. Record stores specializing in this music abounded in the ghettos of major cities. Bobby's Records and Kenny's Record Shack in Harlem, as well as Leo Mintz's Record Shop in Cleveland and Randy's in Gallatin, Tennessee, were only a few examples. Theatres that presented stage shows featuring black performers became the cultural mecca of the black sound in music. The Schiffman Brothers' Apollo Theatre on 125th Street in Harlem, The Uptown and The Earle in Philadelphia, The Howard in Washington, The Royal in Baltimore, and The State Theatre and Eagle Hall in Hartford were household words in black neighborhoods. "Race music" as it was tagged by the white recording and distributing firms of the late 40's and early 50's, had as one of its forms, a vocal group stylizing that manifested itself in duos, trios, quartets, most frequently quintets and occasionally sextets.

Who were the first groups to sing in the "R&B" style and have their art form so dubiously labelled "race music"? Certainly The Mills Brothers, Ink Spots, Charioteers, Choclateers, Red Caps and Delta Rhythm Boys were the earliest of the successful black groups. The Mills Brothers and Ink Spots even received prime international recognition. However, these vanguards, whose acceptance was vast in the white audience, were in fact, groups who sang white popular songs in a very smooth, "inoffensive" white style. There were two groups which followed The Mills Brothers-Ink Spots era that were successfully able to blend the appeal of the massive white audience with the blues, gospel, jazz and rhythm elements

15

of the black musical medium. Even though these two major
pioneers were the first to gain popular acceptance as Rhythm
and Blues vocal groups, their repertoires were somewhat
identifiable to whites.

The first quartet, although at times a quintet, to es-
tablish itself in this mode was the originator of the bird-
named groups. The Ravens were a Harlem based group whose
harmonies were deeply rooted in popular and blues traditions
and whose hopes and aspirations rested on the earlier international successes of The Ink Spots and Mills Brothers.
The Ravens were able to blend smooth vocal accompaniment
with the unique solo artistry of their basso profundo,Jimmy
Ricks and thrush-like tenor lead, Maithe Marshall.Discovered
in a Harlem bar in 1945,Ricks and his singing partner,Warren
Suttles,joined with Leonard Puzey and Ollie Jones[1] and later
at different times with Bill Jennings,Marshall,Joe Medlin,
Tommy Evans and Paul and James Van Loan.[2]

Through the business and musical talents of William San-
ford and Howard Biggs,the group was introduced to Hub Records, where on July 1, 1946,their first recording was released. "Honey"/"Lullabye" (Hub 3030) was followed by two
other releases before the group went to National Records
in 1947 where they recorded 42 sides,mostly in the popular
vein as witnessed by "September Song" (National 9053) and
"Count Every Star" (National 9111).The cohesiveness of The
Ravens' membership was however,shortlived.Maithe Marshall
left to sing with The Marshalls on Savoy and The Bells on
Rama while other members reportedly recorded as the Mercury
version of The Chestnuts.Nat Margo, who still manages the
group,said that the international successes of The Ravens
were continued later by Ricks,Joe Van Loan,Lou Frazier and
Jim Stewart,as they toured Hawaii for 18 weeks and Europe
with Benny Goodman.

The Ravens were the originators of three facets of Rhythm
and Blues group singing that endured throughout the golden
era of the street corner group during the 1950's. Maithe
Marshall and later Joe Van Loan began the inclusion of the
sweet,very high natural and falsetto lead on ballads.Mar-
shall's soaring soprano-like effects on "White Christmas"
and "Silent Night" have remained classics of the high tenor
art. The Ravens' "White Christmas" was the predecessor of
the be-bop edition of the song popularized in 1954 by the
Drifters' and Diablos' heavier versions.The most important
Rhythm and Blues foundation laid by The Ravens,was the featuring of a bass lead.No other group had ever been success-

fully and continuously led by a bass singer.Jimmy Ricks, noted for "Ol' Man River" and "Green Eyes",was often duplicated but never,ever equalled by Bobby Nunn of The Robins and Coasters, Will "Dub" Jones of The Cadets and Coasters and Bill Brown of The Dominoes and Checkers.Unintentionally, The Ravens set the stage for the "bird group era", a disparaging tag for the golden era of the group sound.The Ravens were followed by The Orioles, Flamingos, Swallows, Crows, Robins, Cardinals, Hollywood Blue Jays, Penguins, Meadowlarks,Pelicans, Swans, Wrens, Larks, and Sparrows,to name only a few.

The Ravens,whose famous recordings spanned two decades are remembered for "Ol' Man River", "Write Me A Letter", "Summertime", "Green Eyes",and "A Simple Prayer".In 1971, they were still performing as Ricks and Warren had reformed briefly with two veteran R&B harmony men, Gregory Carroll from The Four Buddies and Orioles,and Jimmy Breedlove from The Cues.

Although The Ravens were the first "race" group to attain some national and international fame,they were not the first to achieve the status of placing a hit record in the top twenty of Billboard Magazine's national pop chart. In August, 1953, a song called "Crying In The Chapel" (Jubilee 5122) entered the sacred realm of Billboard's pop listing and by September 9, 1953,had climbed as high as number fourteen. This was the first time that a song recorded by a black group singing black received national popular recognition. The honor belonged to an often imitated group that was credited with popularizing the "bird" group craze perhaps even more so than their predecessors, The Ravens. The group that is given the most credit for inspiring the Rhythm and Blues quartets and quintets of the 1950's was The Orioles.While The Ravens were originators of the bass lead and high tenor second lead, their reputation was still based on nearly white interpretations of white swing material.The Orioles, on the other hand, interpreted the white material in the style of black free harmony. They recorded such songs as "Dare To Dream" and "I'd Rather Have You Under The Moon" for the general public but in their own style.The Orioles were the innovators of what has become known as pure Rhythm and Blues four part ballad harmony;a mellow,smooth,soft second tenor lead,a blending baritone featured as a "gravel gertie" second lead,a floating high first tenor and a dominant bass. These four vocal parts made up the most innovative of all the R&B groups.

The birth of the Orioles can be traced to the often reported and now famous,Deborah Chessler story.Upon returning
home to Baltimore from military service in 1946,Earlington
(Sonny Til) Tilghman's girlfriend persuaded him to enter an
amateur talent show at a local club.Much to his surprise,
Sonny won first prize on two successive Wednesday nights and
began harmonizing with subsequent winners who were personal
friends and members of the band.

Tommy Gaither(guitarist),George Nelson(baritone), Alexander Sharp (first tenor), Johnny Reed (bass and bassist)
and Sonny, nicknaming themselves The Vibranairs,continued
to sing on local street corners.One night,while harmonizing
on the corners of Pennsylvania and Pitcher Streets in Baltimore,The Vibranairs (not to be confused with TheVibranaires
from Asbury Park,New Jersey -After Hours and Chariot labels)
were invited to sing inside the bar located on that Baltimore
street corner. Inside they were discovered by Deborah Chessler
who had written a song called "It's Too Soon To Know".She
coached and rehearsed the group at her house while they continued to do local gigs in Baltimore.In 1948, she managed
to get them a spot on the Arthur Godfrey Talent Scouts Show.
The penniless Vibranairs,travelled to New York City and in
circumstances that were to haunt other R&B groups on the Godfrey show for years to come,finished second to young George
Shearing. Broke and defeated, The Vibranairs returned to
Baltimore.The next day friends in Baltimore notified them
that Godfrey, impressed by the group's performance, was
interested in having them on his morning show.During their
engagement with Godfrey,the group met Jerry Blaine.The group
was renamed for the Maryland state bird as Blaine recorded
their original rendition of "It's Too Soon To Know" on his
Natural label in the summer of 1948.The side was a modest
R&B hit covered later that summer by The Ravens on National.[3]
The white media immediately categorized The Orioles' release
as "race music":"a new vocal quintette on a new disc that
speeds right into the top spot of the race discs..."[4]

In August, 1948, Blaine renamed his recording company,
Jubilee,relabelling "It's Too Soon To Know" and releasing
"Dare To Dream" in November. This marked the beginning of
a prolific recording career that saw at least 45 records cut
for Jubilee.On virtually every record, Til would close his
eyes,think beautiful thoughts and emit that beautiful crooning tenor.Sonny Til and The Orioles, as Jubilee later decided to bill them,were the pioneers of the big stage acts
to cram big city theatres.Like Frank Sinatra but appealing

to a different audience,they too packed the New York Paramount in the late forties and early fifties.The Orioles had a special appeal to women much more so than any other R&B group. Perhaps it was the romantic way Til bent his body while singing on stage of the haunting melodies accompanied by Gaither's blues guitar or later Charles Harris' clean and simple piano work. "Don't Tell Her What's Happened To Me" (Jubilee 5065) was an example of these prime Orioles' ingredients that conveyed the beauty of people together in the entanglements of life amidst concrete and steel. "I Cover The Waterfront" was similar with George Nelson's added baritone on the bridge. The Orioles' harmony in their second biggest smash "What Are You Doing New Year's Eve" was a little different;the background tended to blend together more uniformly in an almost high pitched closed mouth unison where each member sang the same note instead of complimentary notes. This style had some influence on the later more "rock 'n' rollish" ballad groups such as The Flamingos ("Golden Teardrops", "I'll Be Home"). The "doo-doo-doo" bridge on "New Year's Eve" was duplicated years later by The Flamingos ("Time Was") when they too were recording standards for End. The Orioles were not a group to forget their gospel roots with songs of a religious flavor,"Oh Holy Night","Robe of Calvary" and "In The Mission of St. Augustine". The best Orioles' records as far as the group's sensitive ability to feel its way through a song was concerned were:"Tell Me So", "So Much", "Moonlight","I Miss You So" and "In The Chapel In The Moonlight".

What made The Orioles sing in such a way that was all their own? Why didn't they just simply sing like everyone else?They grew up in a neighborhood where the idols of success were The Ink Spots,The Mills Brothers,and the supposed first but obscure Rhythm and Blues vocal group,Austin Powell and The Cats and The Fiddle (Decca and Manor). When they began singing on Pitcher and Pennsylvania, The Vibranairs intended on singing like the Ink Spots.Alexander Sharp had a very high tenor voice and whenever they sang,he would go into a high tenor range on top of the rest of the harmony. Til tried to get him back into straight harmony,but Sharp could not adjust.The group decided it was better to leave Sharp alone,giving them the style of the first tenor vocal variations on top.Plus they had George Nelson doing second tenor and/or baritone.George would come in at the channel as lead with the harshness in his voice that made The Orioles' bridges famous. Sonny would do the sweet lead and Johnny Reed filled in at the bottom vocally,combining with the rest to form the Orioles' style. George Nelson, as well as all The Orioles, idolized The Ink Spots. They got the idea of the harsh baritone channel from The Ink Spots' baritone who did the same on "If I Didn't Care".George's voice, however, was not a put-on - that was the way he felt. Nelson was a very high strung, sensitive person,who had a deep feeling for music.His appreciation for Louis Armstrong also helped develop his style as the genius of the early baritone leads.

By the winter of 1949-50,The Orioles were the top R&B vocal group in the country.Later they were on the "Star Night" show with Perry Como and Nat "King" Cole,reaching the pinnacle of their career.As most successful acts were compelled to do in the fifties' era, The Orioles were obliged to do those endless strings of one-nighters from The Howard in Washington to The Apollo in New York to The Paradise Hotel in Detroit to The Regal in Chicago and back to The Strand Theatre in New York City.It was somewhere along this lonesome road of one-nighters, that The Orioles were involved in a serious automobile accident,killing Tommy Gaither and seriously injuring George Nelson and Johnny Reed. Also in the car was The Orioles' valet, Sonny Woods,a founding member of The Royals/Midnighters who originated "Moonrise","Every Beat of My Heart","Work With Me Annie" and "The Twist".That automobile crash had far reaching effects on the world of Rhythm and Blues music.The Orioles ceased long distance driving, returning Woods to his native Detroit where he joined The Royals who recorded an Orioles-like "Moonrise". They also did "Every Beat Of My Heart",the predecessor of the hit that launched the career of Gladys Knight and The Pips,who were also from Detroit. After a name change to The Midnighters because of a legal dispute with The Five Royales (Apollo), their "Work With Me Annie" and ensuing suggestive "Annie" records caused a furor in the music business, paving the way for the watered down version of "Roll With Me Henry" (an answer to Midnighters' lead singer Henry Ballard) by Etta James, which was diluted further by Georgia Gibbs' "Dance With Me Henry". Chubby Checker later recorded Hank Ballard and The Midnighters'original of "The Twist", starting a whole new Rock 'n' Roll dance craze in the early sixties.

The Orioles,on the other hand,were never quite the same after the fatal crash."Oh Holy Night" was the last record by the strictly original Orioles. In August, 1951, Ralph Williams became the new guitarist on "I Miss You So". The song,however, was not a tribute to Gaither.The group paid homage to their quiet organizer in the ensuing "Pal Of Mine".

When they recorded the song in June,1951,The Orioles broke up in the studio at just the thought of Gaither and the accident."Happy Go Lucky Blues" was recorded as the flip side to compensate for the grim reminder.Some of The Orioles then started having trouble making gigs and maintaining their interest in singing.George Nelson was occasionally replaced by Ralph Williams on vocals.In 1953,either before or after the recording of "Crying In The Chapel",the group reorganized and became a vocal quintet with Til,Sharp,Reed,Charlie Harris on vocals and piano, Gregory Carroll,who came from The Four Buddies (Savoy) to replace Nelson and Ralph Williams on guitar. This group lasted until 1954 when The Orioles, no longer getting good material to record,were losing competitively on the personal appearance market to the dawn of the Rock 'n' Roll group era.There were so many new young groups in 1954, that agents could provide four groups for the price of the superstar Orioles. A third Orioles group was formed in the fall of 1954,right after the release of Jubilee 5161. This group finished out the Jubilee series ending with a redoing of "Don't Go To Strangers",5 but by now,their sound had changed.Harmony was no longer considered important as the harder beat of tenor and baritone saxes cracked through "I Love You Mostly".These new Orioles were however,a really sound harmony group. Til had discovered them at The Apollo, singing modern harmony under the name of The Regals.The Regals who became the revitalized Orioles, were a good club act but could not attain the previous successes of the prior Orioles.All of The Regals,except lead singer "Sonny" Wright,finished the Jubilee recordings and then moved on to Vee-Jay. The biggest record for Billie Adams, Gerald Holman, Albert "Diz" Russell, Jerry "Texas" Rodriquez,Til and accompanist Paul Griffin was "Happy 'Til The Letter".That was the end of The Orioles as a forceful fifties group.6

In the 1960's and 1970's,Til tried several comebacks with other Orioles groups that he formed. He recorded an album for Charley Parker in 1962 with Gerald Gregory of The Spaniels and two neighborhood Philadelphians from The Castelles, tenor Delton "Satan" McCall,and baritone Billy Taylor.Another very well done album for RCA in 1971,included Bobby Thomas and Mike Robinson of the After-Hours Vibranaires who had met Sonny long before at The Royal in Baltimore.

In retrospect,The Orioles had a meaningful impact on the sound of Rhythm and Blues groups in the fifties.The Orioles' R&B treatment of pop standards developed a trend in American music that has continued to the present day."Till Then" was repeated in the R&B vein by The Classics in the early sixties. "Hold Me, Thrill Me, Kiss Me" (Mel Carter), "Secret Love" (Doris Day,Moonglows)" and "I Cover The Waterfront" (Diana Ross) were all prime examples.In their heyday,The Orioles hung out in Washington and Baltimore with many famous groups from that area;The Swallows,Heartbreakers,Marylanders,and Cardinals.Til taught The Marylanders (Jubilee) how to sing. The Cardinals' first record,"Shouldn't I Know" (Atlantic) included The Orioles' trademark of the floating tenor and hoarse baritone second lead.The Swallows' guitarist, Fred "Money" Johnson,employed the strumming blues effect of Tommy Gaither.Bobby Thomas of The Vibranaires sounded just like Til in 1954.Nate Nelson,the second great lead of The Flamingos was a sweet sounding,emotionally cracking tenor similar to Sonny Til.

The Orioles have lived on forever in the minds of many singers who ever attempted group harmony.They recorded standards because they believed that the feeling emitted on a song was more important than the originality of the material. Perhaps that is what killed them.The new Orioles (Regals) fell apart because they could not get new material,as the recording of pop standards became passe in the mid-fifties. The fact that they all lived in different cities (New York, Philadelphia,Detroit) prevented any meaningful rehearsals necessary to the cohesiveness that held the early group together.

Another forceful pioneer group that began four years after the Orioles in 1950,similarly using the tenor and baritone leads was a group out of Newport News,Virginia,the legendary Five Keys.Like The Orioles,they too recorded standards at first but had much more sensational success with such original material as "Ling Ting Tong" and "Close Your Eyes".Unlike The Orioles,they had a modest collection of four million selling hit records; the Rhythm and Blues version of "Glory Of Love" (Aladdin) in 1951,the rock and rolling "Ling Ting Tong" (Capitol) in 1954 and the big band sounding,pop stylized smashes of 1956,"Out Of Sight,Out Of Mind" (Capitol)and "Wisdom Of A Fool", (Capitol).

While attending high school in 1950,two sets of brothers began imitating The Orioles in churches and on the corners of "Two-five and Jay" (Twenty-fifth Street and Jefferson Avenue) in their hometown of Newport News, Virginia. The Sentimental Four,Rudy and Bernie West and Raphael (Rayfield) and Ripley Ingram,entered an amateur program at The Jefferson

Theatre. They were told that the winner of any three consecutive Wednesday night programs would automatically be invited to enter the famous amateur night contests at The Apollo in New York. Winning every single contest in Newport News hands down, they went on to be victorious at The Apollo Theatre, besting some thirty-one contestants. They were then invited to a week's engagement at both The Royal and Howard. As they established themselves along the Eastern seaboard, they were heard by Eddie Mesner, owner of a West Coast label, Aladdin. At the time that they were signed by Aladdin, Raphael Ingram entered the armed services and was replaced by Maryland Pierce from The Avalons and Dickie Smith. In turn, when Raphael Ingram returned home, he joined The Avalons, a local group whose harmonies closely resembled his brother's group.

The name was changed from The Sentimental Four to The Five Keys, but the implication of the prior name, singing sweet love songs in a quiet, romantic, earthy way, was not altered. The Keys added a sixth man, piano player Joe Jones and set out on tours that covered both coasts. This is a possible reason why some of The Keys' Aladdin sides were recorded in Los Angeles. Most of The Keys' studio work was done in New York as it was easier to come up from Virginia to Mesner's offices in New York, than it was to go to Los Angeles. It was on one of those West Coast tours from Los Angeles to Seattle in 1952 when they recorded "How Long", "I Cried For You" and others.[7]

The Five Keys' first successes were patterned after The Orioles' innovative trademark but that is where the similarity ended. While Til's tenor crooned, West's pitched and rang sharply and clearly as a bell backed by harmony without the stand-out bass; a harmony that could send waves tingling through any spine. Dickie Smith came very close to imitating George Nelson on the baritone second lead. After "Glory Of Love", this double lead treatment was given to many pop standards including "How Long", "Someday Sweetheart", "Red Sails In The Sunset" and "Yes Sir, That's My Baby". Smith also had solo leads on "With A Broken Heart" which he wrote, "When You're Gone" and "Ghost Of A Chance". The down home blues songs that separated The Keys from their predecessors were led by Maryland Pierce; "Hucklebuck With Jimmy", "My Saddest Hour" and "Serve Another Round". It is ironic that it was to be this type of song with more of an uptempo novelty element added in the form of "Ling Ting Tong" that was to really bring The Keys to national status in 1954.

In 1953, both Smith and Rudy West had entered the army and were replaced by Ramon Loper and Ulysses K. Hicks, respectively.Both Pierce and Rudy West have said at different times that Hicks had a versatile voice ranging from bass to tenor.It is not actually known what records he sang on but he was in the background on "Ling Ting Tong",the catchy jump tune with the oriental percussion and impossible to spell lyric,"Tais-a-moke-um-boot-ah-yay".Besides Hicks,the group on "Ling Ting Tong" included Pierce (lead), Ripley Ingram (octave tenor),Ramon Loper (baritone) and Bernard West(bass).

Hicks suddenly died in 1954 before Rudy West returned home. The lead tenor position was temporarily filled by Dickie Smith's cousin from New York City, Willie Winfield of The Harptones.Winfield's group had become a success in New York, shortening his stay with The Keys. However, to this day, there has never been another lead tenor who could be called the closest thing to Rudy West except Willie Winfield.When he was in Virginia,Winfield probably spread a good word about the company for which he had been recording. When Dickie Smith returned from the service in the winter of 1954-55, he left The Keys to record on his own for Bruce Records.He re-recorded "When You're Gone" presumably backed up by The Harptones.

The Five Keys were the first Rhythm and Blues vocal group to record with a major record company, resulting in financial success and high quality recordings.The Keys' manager,Sol Richfield,was lucky enough to know Dave Cavanaugh at Capitol when the company was planning to expand into the Rhythm and Blues field.Luckily,The Five Keys were in the right place at the right time.They were also lucky to be backed up by the Howard Biggs (former Ravens' arranger) Orchestra and to be recorded by Capitol's advanced audio techniques.No one could ever say that The Keys made a bad record for Capitol. Each of the Capitol releases had that studio fresh vocal and instrumental quality.

Although many R&B purists consider the Aladdin material as the pearl of The Five Keys' repertoire, Aladdin, a small independent,with limited recording assets,could never have reproduced the sound of The Five Keys as Capitol did. The vocal group lead singer's lead singer, Rudy West, sounded incredibly clear.Every note hit pure perfection as West was backed by that luxuriously silky smooth harmony.When West did return from the army,he answered Maryland Pierce on what has got to be the greatest high tenor echo record ever made, "Close Your Eyes". This song was so highly regarded that it was recorded by The Admirals on King and in 1967,by Peaches and Herb."Gee Whittakers" and "Don't You Know I Love You", followed as the group's versatility on singing fast songs

24

was concentrated on by radio stations. More than any other songs, these two typified The Keys' professional attempts at singing "doo-wop", a special type of R&B harmony that was becoming big in 1955. Even The Cardinals, a strictly ballad group were "a-doo-doo-wop" and "a-doo-doo-wanging" their way through "Come Back My Love" in 1955. This "doo-wop" craze, however, neglected "Cause You're My Lover" and "I Wish I'd Never Learned To Read", as two unheralded Five Keys' ballad gems of that year. The big break for The Keys came when the group and the label decided to adapt The Keys' style to the big band sound. "Out Of Sight, Out Of Mind" and "Wisdom of A Fool" were beautifully done masterpieces, replacing the days of the piano-drums-bass-sax combos at Aladdin and early Capitol. Unfortunately, The Keys may have lost something by 1956, as the group on both of these hits was overdubbed with a female chorus. None of their ensuing ten records ever attained this popularity again and in 1958, Rudy West, who had grown tired of one-nighters, producers, managers, agents and song writers, decided he had had enough.

The group then consisting of Dickie Smith (baritone), Ramon Loper (tenor), Maryland Pierce (lead and second tenor), Dickie Threat (lead and first tenor) and Bernie West (bass), went to King Records in 1960, to record some very good fifties type ballads. The group could not make it without Rudy, who recorded on his own for King. In 1962, Rudy West, trying his hand at producing, re-did "Out Of Sight", with a new group, cutting the master with Jack Kerr. This edition of The Five Keys included Rudy, Bernie West, John Boyd, Willie Friday, and Dickie Smith. In 1965, the same duo produced "No Matter" with Rudy, Edmond Hall, Ollie Sidney, Theodore Jones and George Winfield. Both of these attempts, distributed by Segway and Inferno Records respectively, flopped - "no money honey".[8] This same group, some of whose members recorded as The Chateaus, has been appearing today on the revival circuit. Another group with Jones, Pierce, Gene Moore, Ray Haskins and Ramon Loper, had done the oldies routine, in the major black theatres in the mid-sixties.

A pioneer group whose acceptance as black artists was not as wide as The Five Keys, was the so-called Alan Freed group, The Moonglows. In 1951, vocalist Bobby Lester and piano player Harvey Fuqua, had grown tired of the amateur show routine in Louisville, Kentucky. They piled into Lester's '49 Oldsmobile, heading for the greener pastures of Cleveland, Ohio, where Fuqua's pal, Alexander "Pete" Graves was living. In Cleveland, the three formed a new group called The Crazy

Sounds,with quitarist Billy Johnson,and bass singer,Prentiss Barnes, the brother of James "Pookie" Hudson of The Spaniels from Gary,Indiana.They met a young Blues and Rhythm disc jockey,Alan Freed,at Radio Station WJW in Cleveland, who was starting his own label, Champagne.Freed's program, The Moondog Show,which played basically heavy blues,was the first of its kind to bring the music to all teenaged listeners.

Freed had been gaining national recognition with his live stage shows in Ohio.Featuring The Swallows,Edna McGriff and The Buddy Lucas Orchestra,Freed drew over 5,000 admissions to The Crystal Beach Ballroom in Lorraine,The Summit Beach Ballroom in Akron and The Avon Oaks Ballroom in Youngstown, Ohio in June of 1952. By September of that year,Freed had managed to obtain a five city hook-up with Detroit,Columbus, Chicago,Pittsburgh,and New York (via WNJR in Newark).[9]Freed however was not the only disc jockey playing the so-called Blues and Rhythm, or "race" records.

Although Freed had been credited with exposing white teenagers to the "new" music,there were other disc jockeys who had long been playing the music over primarily black oriented stations. Bruce Payne, the "jet pilot of jive" on WBCO in Birmingham; Andy Franklin on WSRS in Cleveland;Larry Dean Faulkner of "Larry Leaps In" on WERD in Nashville; Rufus Thomas over WDIA in Memphis;Nipsey Russell,a former MC of the Amateur Show at The Apollo and Phil Gordon,the original "Dr. Jive" on WLIB in New York; Tommy Smalls,the new "Dr. Jive" on WWRL in New York;Vernon "Dr. Daddy-O" Winslow on WMRY in New Orleans; Abram Ross on KLPR in Oklahoma City; Douglass "Jocko" Henderson and Ramon Bruce on WHAT in Philadelphia; and Chester "Daddy Yo Hot Rod" McDowell on KCIJ in Shreveport, were some of the jocks playing R&B when it was still considered "race" music. With the exception of perhaps, Smalls, Bruce,and Henderson,none of them continued successfully into the Rock 'n' Roll era.

Freed liked The Crazy Sounds,recorded them for Champagne and changed the name to The Moonglows to fit into his Moondog Show. Their first record, a hundred dollar collectors item today,"Just Can't Tell No Lie" / "I've Been Your Dog (Ever Since I've Been Your Man)",was allegedly written by Freed under the pseudonymn,Al Lance.Freed then introduced the group to Art Sheridan and Steve Chandler,co-owners of Chance Records in Chicago.At the time, Ewart Abner worked for Chance.He later became one of the founders of VeeJay, Abner and Falcon Records. The Moonglows recorded five records for Chance, the same label that pioneered with The

26

Spaniels and The Flamingos. All bu. "Secret Love" were written by Alan Freed and Harvey Fuqua. The most famous Moonglows' record of all,"Sincerely",was written by Bobby Lester,whose name did not appear on the label at all.[10]Except for "Secret Love", The Moonglows' Chance sides were rough and crude,setting the stage for group harmonies that were to come in later years. Fuqua warbled through things like "I Was Wrong","Whistle My Love" and "219 Train".Occasionally,he would shift into the harmony with the two tenors, Graves and Lester, leaving a partial lead to bass,Barnes. Although they were not the first to do it,this was the beginning of the prominent doo-wop bass; "yay-yay-ah", "let me hear yuh whistle" and "ooh-wahh"! This was pure street corner singing but it had advanced in that it was backed up by the sax honking staccato of Red Holloway's Orchestra. After their version of "Secret Love",high pitched harmony followed by Lester's rough ballad lead and Barnes' doo-wop bass, The Moonglows had had it with Chance Records. Even though their record was a nationwide R&B hit in the summer and fall of 1954,Chance told them that their record was doing poorly.Fuqua and Lester who had to moonlight their recording careers by working in a coal yard - Harvey drove, Bobby shovelled-influenced the rest of the group to leave Chance. They went to Phil Chess,whom they had previously met with Freed at WJW.[11]They began recording in the fall of 1954 as two groups,The Moonglows for Chess and The Moonlighters for Checker.The Moonlighters were definitely a pun intended as Bobby and Harvey sang duets, supported by the rest of the group on up-tempo tunes that had a rolling,doo-wop almost Latin flavor, "Shoo-Doo-Be-Doo (My Loving Baby)" and "Hug And A Kiss" in 1954.

While The Moonglows were moonlighting as The Moonlighters on Checker, they recorded a song called "Sincerely", that established precedents that were to become known as The Moonglows' harmony;the prominent bass beginning,the forceful, crying, pleading, tenor lead,the smooth high pitched blow harmony of the background and the distinctive "ooh-wah" ending.But The Moonglows just weren't oohing and wahing,they sounded as if they were actually blowing into the microphone. This sound was rich,lusty and much more polished than what the group had emitted on the previous Chance recordings.It made them the black tie and tails class group of the era, a model that was to be emulated but very seldom equalled in the course of Rhythm and Blues from 1954 on.Only one group, The Dells,ever managed to successfully duplicate the sound and later capitalize on it commercially in the late sixties and seventies. The Moonglows were The Dells' poppas in 1956 when the latter was just beginning as The El Rays for Chess. Marvin Junior, Chuck Barksdale, Vern Allison, and Mike McGill were a very crude singing group who were taught the intricacies of delicate harmony balance while hanging out in front of the Chess offices on South Michigan Avenue in Chicago. When The Dells moved across the street to Vee Jay, adding tenor Jerry Funches, they became the successor to The Moonglows, beginning with "Tell The World", "Oh What A Night" and "Why Do You Have To Go". In the sixties, when The Dells returned to Chess/Cadet and replaced Funches with former Flamingos' great, Johnny Carter, their status as The Moonglows' disciples became obvious on "Stay In My Corner", "Nadine", "The Love That Stays On My Mind" and "Open Up My Heart". Although Junior's voice has changed to an earthier, grittier version of his earlier exciting tenor, The Dells today are the one solid example of how a street corner fifties group had the courage of its convictions to continue to pursue singing as they saw fit. It is a joy to see a group such as The Dells grow and mature artistically when so many others had grown discouraged after only a few recordings.

After "Sincerely", The Moonglows blow-noted their way through "Most Of All", "In My Diary", "We Go Together", "When I'm With You", "Blue Velvet", "The Beating Of My Heart", and "Starlite". All of these records had the same basic Moonglows' ingredients except "Most Of All", "Diary", and "Starlite"/"In Love", where the melody, rough and stuttering, was highlighted by the soaring falsetto of "Pete" Graves. These were very catchy rock 'n' roll ballads that added to the Moonglows' versatility. Only on the easy rocker "See Saw" and the mellow "Please Send Me Someone To Love" (written by Percy Mayfield), did The Moonglows return to the earthier lead stylings of Harvey Fuqua.

The charisma of Alan Freed and the frenzied following he created could not do much to enhance the financial success of The Moonglows in the fifties. Both "Sincerely" and "Most Of All" were recorded shortly after by The McGuire Sisters with "Sincerely" being a million seller. The Moonglows never really escaped the category of R&B, selling a trifling by comparison, 300,000 copies of "Sincerely". Only in the Fall of 1958, when the group was renamed Harvey and The Moonglows did it achieve real success with "The Ten Commandments Of Love", a monologue echoed by sugary bass and billowed by the finest example of their blow harmony notes. Right after this

28

the group began to disintegrate. Harvey entered the production and arrangement end of the business, first with some of The Moonglows and later with a young Detroit group called The Spinners. Henry Fambrough, Billy Henderson, Bobby Smith, and Pervis Jackson (excluding Edgar "Chico" Edwards) are four of the originals who today are selling millions of records for Atlantic. At different times but most notably on "Twelve Months Of The Year", (a song Harvey did as a single backed up by a group), a young Detroit singer, Marvin Gaye, participated in the background vocal work. As late as 1964, "Pete" Graves tried to resurrect The Moonglows with George Thorpe and Bearle Ashton from The Velvets and Dock Green from The Five Crowns in New York City for the Lana and Times Square labels. Today, Lester, Graves, Fuqua, (on records only), plus Doc Williams and Chuck Lewis are back creating new items ("Sincerely '72" and "You've Chosen Me") and redoing the old classics.

The Ravens, Orioles, Five Keys, and Moonglows were the pioneers of a neglected music that later mushroomed into the booming golden era of the vocal group when it seemed that every independent record label had a stable of dozens of groups. Only The Flamingos from Chicago and The Clovers from Washington, D.C. (Harold Lucas, Matthew McQuintar, Harold Winley, John "Buddy" Bailey and guitarist Billy Harris) can be added to this hard core of courageous, innovative groups. The ballad harmonies of The Flamingos and the black blues orientations of The Clovers were new elements that were added to the foundation built by the four pioneers. The only ingredient that these six founding fathers had not added to the potpourri of the black vocal sound in music was the influence of the gospel choir singer.

[1]Ollie Jones later sang with The Blenders (Decca). His real claim to fame came as lead singer of The Cues (Capitol and Prep).Their best records included "Burn That Candle", "Destination Twenty-One Hundred and Sixty-Five" and "Crazy, Crazy Party".The rest of the group included Eddie Barnes, Jimmy Breedlove,Robey Kirkland and Abel DeCosta who was also with The Blenders. Under the stage name, Winfield Scott, Kirkland wrote many songs for The Five Keys (Capitol) and LaVern Baker (Atlantic). The Cues began as The Cabineers (three guys, one girl) backing up Bing Crosby in the style of The Delta Rhythm Boys.They signed as a studio group for Atlantic backing up Ivory Joe Hunter,LaVern Baker,Ruth Brown and Big Joe Turner,recording under the names of The Ivorytones, The Gliders, The Rhythm Makers,and The Blues Kings respectively.When they recorded for Capitol they had to use another name,The Cues,for contract reasons. Interview with Eddie Barnes,July 31, and August 1,1971.

[2]Jack Sbarbori,"The Ravens", Record Exchanger, Vol. 2, number 4.

[3]Sonny Til interviewed by Tom Luciani and Joe Marchesani, WFUV-FM, May 7, 1964.

[4]Cash Box, August 21, 1948.

[5]Marvin Goldberg, "Biography: The Orioles", Record Exchanger,Vol. 2, number 3.

[6]Much of the preceding information is taken from personal conversations had by Sal Mondrone with Sonny Til,1970-71.

[7]Interview with Rudy West, June 28, 1972.

[8]Interview with Theodore Jones, June 28,1972.

[9]Billboard,June 7,1952,page 34 and July 5,1952,page 21.

[10]Harvey Fuqua and Bobby Lester interviewed by Bim Bam Boom, September 10,1971.

[11]Bobby Lester interviewed by Gus Gossert,WPIX-FM,November 21, 1971.

Chapter 3

Gospel On The Stoops Of New York

By 1950, the successes of The Ink Spots,The Ravens and The Orioles, had become significant examples of the black man making it in the music business.Thanks to the embryonic appearance of recording companies specializing in the black market (Negro markets as referred to by the music trade magazines), a sure fire way for young people to have fun, gain valued neighborhood prestige and possibly make some money,was to be discovered by a record company businessman and record either an old standard or a favorite neighborhood street song.Ready made audiences could easily be found as groups of young men harmonized as they stood on a neighborhood street corner,huddled in a hallway,or congregated in an old alley way. These street corner troubadors could easily simulate the effects of an echo chamber in a stair well, subway entrance or school lavatory.

As teenage appreciation for The Ravens and Orioles swelled, public respect for labels like National and Jubilee and later for Aladdin,Savoy, King,and its subsidiary Federal, also increased. Singing at night on your own private Harlem street corner in the shadow of The Apollo Theatre was just a good time. Taking a stab at a taste of show business on Wednesday night's amateur program became an exciting risk, but the promises of signing a recording contract,becoming a star, hearing your own records on the radio,having your girl friend telephone a local disc jockey to request your record and making some money,created dreams that staggered the imagination.Rhythm and Blues music barked out from loud speakers in local record shops, talent shows were run in school auditoriums,radio stations sponsored out-door talent searches, dances were held in community centers and churches,and battles of the groups,open competition among vocal groups,could be seen and heard in parks along Morningside Drive and Convent Avenue in New York City.The successes of The Ravens and Orioles,at first tempted many an adolescent. The music blaring in the street and the backstage autograph seekers at The Apollo were signs of the new phenomenon. The street corner was the proving ground. The true test of how well a man could feel a note was how well he performed on the street with his buddies.

Four youngsters who had learned to sing in the churches of Durham, North Carolina, would gather on the brownstone stoops of their homes on 127th and 131st Streets to listen to the radio and harmonize. These four young men, James Baldwin;his two brothers,Wilmer and David; and a fourteen year old,Clyde McPhatter, sang gospel music in its purist form while not necessarily imitating The Ravens and Orioles. They would take part in a battle of songs at what was called the "Madison Square Garden of Harlem",The Golden Gate Ballroom on 7th Avenue, where groups from all over the metropolitan area would compete including The Golden Gate Quartet, The Brooklyn Crusaders,The Selah Jubilee Singers,The Harmony Five and The Thrasher Wanderers (Wonders).The Baldwin Brothers and Clyde McPhatter toured professionally as a gospel quartet, The Mount Lebanon Singers in fests of song throughout the East Coast.[1]

At the same time,a young music student who had graduated from The Juilliard School of Music, had been persuaded to start a vocal group of his own by songwriter-manager,Rose Marks.Billy Ward,who had become the vocal coach and pianist for a group called The Ques,was looking for a lead singer to imitate the plush high tenor sounds of Bill Kenny of The Ink Spots.A member of The Ques,Joe Lamont,had been a member .of another spiritual group that had battled against The Mount Lebanon Singers.He told Billy Ward that there was a high pitched kid uptown who really knew how to wail.McPhatter figured that he could seriously make some money instead of just singing on stoops and in church. McPhatter's parents being deeply religious, wanted Clyde to have no part in any so-called popular Rhythm and Blues singing.In spite of his parents, McPhatter entered an Apollo amateur contest, won and then he and his friend , Charlie White, took the train downtown to audition for Billy Ward.Ward created an entirely new group,The Dominoes,around the spiritual lead of Clyde McPhatter. The Dominoes then went on to rewrite American popular music history.They went on the Arthur Godfrey Show as a spiritual group, and won first prize. They later appeared with The Orioles at The Apollo,again as a spiritual group.It was at this Apollo show in 1950,that The Dominoes, billed as an up and coming spiritual group,dressed in their raggedy blue jackets and grey pants,were able to blend the roots of gospel and blues together into a distinctive sound[2] Their music also had a trace of jubilee which was a raucous style of church singing more spontaneous and improvisational than the more contrived call and response patterns of spiritual gospel music. There were other milestones.They popularized the bass lead format, introduced by The Ravens, into a hit record,"Sixty Minute Man". They contributed to the popular music world two great lead singers, Clyde McPhatter and Jackie Wilson.

The original Dominoes were Clyde McPhatter (tenor), Charlie White (second tenor), Joe Lamont (baritone), Bill Brown (bass) and Billy Ward (piano).Their harmony on ballads, "When The Swallows Come Back To Capistrano", "Harbor Lights" and the eerie "The Bells", was filled with virile, strong, religious power.When they added a few ooh-wah syllables to their four part harmony on "That's What You're Doing To Me" and "Have Mercy Baby",spiced with hand clapping, shouting,and the honking tenor horn,they rocked,rolled and thrilled the soul of other groups who were to follow their creation of the gospel/blues oriented rock 'n' roll jump tune that later became so important in the mid fifties.

When The Dominoes were in the Federal studios in Cincinnati, at the same time as the rising star, Little Esther Phillips, they recorded at least two songs ("The Deacon Moves In" and "Lookin' For A Man") with her. She, however, was never a member of the group.[3] Two changes did occur in The Dominoes' membership in the Fall and Winter of 1951-52, when Charlie White and Bill Brown left the group. First, White signed with Atlantic as a single and as an addition to The Clovers.Later, White and Brown were induced by King to start a rival group to compete against The Dominoes.[4]

In 1952,Ward replaced Brown and White with David McNiel (bass) from The Larks and James Van Loan(tenor) who later sang with The Ravens. McNiel could be heard bass leading on "Pedal Pushin' Papa". By July, 1952, The Dominoes had become entrenched as one of the top R&B groups in the country as they were credited with the number one selling R&B record for nine consecutive weeks. As R&B was beginning to gain in national popularity, Billboard started devoting four times as many pages to R&B. The Pittsburgh Courier's Theatrical Poll voted The Dominoes as the most popular quartet in the land, over The Five Keys and The Clovers, as they appeared at New York's Carnegie Hall.[5]

Despite all the apparent success,trouble began to brew as Clyde McPhatter began to take his singing seriously: "Whenever I'd get back on the block where everybody'd heard my records...half the time I couldn't even afford a Coca-Cola".[6] McPhatter was being paid a hundred dollars a week salary out of which came $12.00 in taxes,plus food and hotel bills.The star lead singer had no trouble remembering his father telling him that he could make more money downtown in the garment district.Finally,after a gig in Providence, Rhode Island,McPhatter left the group.Clyde stayed around a few weeks to familiarize young Jackie "Sonny" Wilson with the vocal techniques and dance routines of The Dominoes. These two great lead singers and solo performers,however, never performed or recorded together.

McPhatter gathered his few possessions, went home, and waited until Lou Krefetz of Atlantic Records called him. McPhatter met Ahmet Ertegun who suggested that a new group could be built around him. Clyde went back to Harlem and spoke to two brothers who belonged to The Thrasher Wonders, a brother-sister act he used to sing against in church.Gerhart Thrasher(tenor), Andrew "Bubba" Thrasher (baritone), Bill Pinckney (bass) and Charlie White,rehearsed and rehearsed, made one record,until Jesse Stone came up with "Money Honey". It was an instant smash for The Drifters,who incorporated gospel and blues in the same manner as The Dominoes. The best examples of this type of singing were "Gone","The Bells Of St. Mary","What'cha Gonna Do",and "Let The Boogie Woogie Roll". If there was one recording that made The Drifters famous, it was one on which Clyde McPhatter did not sing lead. Bill Pinckney bassed his way through a version of "White Christmas" that had Irving Berlin rolling in his grave", even though black artists had previously given the song a similar treatment. The Drifters had actually added to The Ravens' rendition which in turn was a re-do of the original black version done by The Sentimentalists (Manor 8003) in 1945.[7] By late 1953,The Drifters were soaring and The Dominoes were fading. McPhatter was suddenly drafted. He was replaced briefly in the group by David Baughn,who recorded only two sides for The Drifters in 1955 as Atlantic kept releasing McPhatter led items.Being stationed in Buffalo, New York,McPhatter found it easy to make it back to New York City on weekends to appear at stage shows at The Brooklyn Paramount. On these furloughs,he recorded first with Ruth Brown("Love Has Joined Us Together") and then by himself ("Seven Days"/"I'm Not Worthy Of You"), while still main- taining that cracking clear gospel feeling.When McPhatter finally did return from the service in 1956, he became a single artist recording some of the finest tunes produced during the Rock 'n' Roll era; "Treasure Of Love",the beau- tiful "Without Love" (redone by Tom Jones in 1970),"A Lover's Question"(his biggest seller) and "Can't Stand Up Alone".

34

The Drifters meanwhile regrouped,with Baughn being replaced
by Johnny Moore and guitarist Jimmy Oliver on such mild R&B
hits as "Adorable" and "Soldier Of Fortune". The Drifters
then went through a three year hiatus until 1959,when their
manager, George Treadwell,having a long term contract for
the group to appear at The Apollo, reformed the group entirely around The Crowns,who were Ben E. King,James "Poppa"
Clark,Elsbeary Hobbs,Dock Green and Charles "Charlie Boy"
Thomas. After "There Goes My Baby", The Drifters became a
history unto themselves documented by Bill Millar.

McPhatter continued on his own, having a big hit with
Mercury, "Lover Please" in 1962. He toured Europe in the
mid-sixties before drifting into total obscurity until the
Rock 'n' Roll revival of 1970.Had the right doors been opened
to McPhatter,as they were for other fifties rock 'n' rollers,
he could have been a great star and media personality. However,that was the cruel fate that befell most R&B stars of
the period. On June 13, 1972, the one man who had blended
gospel,blues and rhythm so well into a new music called Rock
'n' Roll had died.David Baughn,Charlie White,and Bill Brown
are gone today,but none has left such an enormous legacy.
It is impossible to list all the lead singers who tried to
imitate Clyde. It is perhaps easy to say that the success
of "Oh Happy Day" by The Edwin Hawkins Singers and Aretha
Franklin's return to gospel in 1972 ("Amazing Grace") are
evidences of McPhatter's gospel pioneering from 1950-57.One
group whose influence from McPhatter is so deep that they
recorded the same songs with the same phrasing,was The Diablos.
How a Detroit group got to be so heavily influenced by an
East coast singer is not easy to trace.Perhaps The Diablos
practiced with McPhatter and The Drifters while they appeared
at The Paradise Theatre in Detroit.The Diablos were famous
for "The Wind",a ghost like ballad that sold well as an oldie,
years after its release in 1954.Consequently,the group never
received what it justly deserved.All their recordings were
made by Fortune Records, whose studios were located in a
garage behind Jack and Devora Brown's record store.The garage
had something to do with the honky-tonk tinny sound of some
of The Diablos' records (others sounded worse).The influence
that McPhatter had on The Diablos and their lead singer,
Nolan Strong, had to be more than just coincidence.Strong
sounded like a weaker,higher pitched example of McPhatter
when he sang "When The Swallows Come Back To Capistrano".
On a 1955 Diablos' hit,"The Way You Dog Me Around",the bass
channel ("the way, mmm, mmm, you have, dogged me around")

was very similar to Bill Brown's ("Baby, come to my arms, mmm,mmm'')on The Dominoes' "I Am With You".As if this wasn't enough,The Drifters' harmony was duplicated on "White Christmas,"What You Gonna Do" and "Someday You'll Want Me To Want You".If it had not been for some of Strong's original material,The Diablos could easily have been a junior Dominoes or Drifters. Why?

In 1954,Nolan Strong,[8]his brother Jimmy, Willie Hunter, Quentin Ewbanks,and guitarist Bob "Chico" Edwards,were attending Detroit's Central High School across the street from the Fortune garage.Nolan had written "The Wind" while the group was hanging out on Hudson and Tillman Streets.While reading a book in school called El Nino Diablo (The Little Devil),Nolan thought of the name Diablos for the group.They were later signed by Fortune when the group just happened to walk into the Fortune studio. Strong had been a vocal student of Billy Ward. Perhaps that is how he learned the lead phrasing and harmony patterns that were so reminiscent of The Dominoes and Drifters.Strong simply blended the soul of his idol,Sonny Til,with the harmonic spiritual soul of The Dominoes and McPhatter into what was known as the original Detroit sound.While in the service,Strong wrote songs including the rocker "If I", and the soothing "Since You're Gone",that the revised group(George Scott replaced Quentin Ewbanks as bass) later recorded as mild R&B hits.[9]

There were other early R&B quartets that also began by singing church music. One group that began battling The Thrasher Wonders and The Selah Jubilee Singers in the churches of Brooklyn,New York, were the relatively unknown Majors. The Majors,who were basically Bernard "Jimmy" Beckum (lead), Scott Alvin(first tenor), Clyde Lee(baritone) and William Bebee(bass),began as part of the resident gospel group of the St. Mark's Holiness Church of New York,where they were occasionally joined by Gene Mumford and Milton Grayson,who later sang with The Dominoes on the pop-rock 'n' roll revivals of "Stardust" and"Deep Purple" in 1956.This group, known as The Brooklyn Crusaders became regulars on the Joe Bostic Gospel Show on WLIB in New York and toured with The Mighty Clouds Of Joy, The Staple Singers,The Caravans,The Soul Stirrers, which featured Sam Cooke,The Zion Kings of Harmony,and The Dixie Hummingbirds.After doing a few programs in Illinois as The Chicago Crusaders,the group changed its style to barbershop and its name tc of all things,The Drifters.They were later discovered while working in Kearney, New Jersey,by an Arthur Godfrey talent scout who had discovered The Chordettes ("Mr. Sandman", "Lollipop"). After

36

finishing second on the Godfrey show, they were taken to Derby Records where another group with Brooklyn gospel roots had been signed.

The Majors recorded four sides for Derby including "Come On Up To My Room" and "You Ran Away With My Heart" written by lead singer Beckum.The former, an uptempo jump included Brownie McGhee,the old blues guitar man on the session.In the winter of 1954-55,another occasional Brooklyn Crusader, David Jones, returned from the service with a tune he had written called "Soldier Boy".Jones had been the lead singer of The Four Fellows on Derby with Jimmy McGowan,Larry Banks and Teddy Williams.Their Derby record of "Bend Of The River"/ "I Tried", had not been much of a success. Jones tried to persuade two reluctant Majors,Beckum and Alvin,to join with him on "Soldier Boy". Derby's A&R man,Phil Rose,who later worked with The Diamonds at Mercury,thought well enough of The Four Fellows that he started another label, Glory, to push the group.The Four Fellows went on to blend their smooth gospel harmonies into a pop style that was a gigantic smash on "Soldier Boy" in 1955.The Four Fellows were undoubtedly ahead of their time,evoking a velvet style that could have been commercial today.Their recording career was,however, short-lived as the public gave only mild reception to their subsequent professional efforts, "You Don't Know Me","Fallen Angel", "Angels Say", and "I Sit In My Window".

Unlike The Dominoes,Drifters,and Four Fellows, The Majors could not successfully transform their gospel foundations into a viable pop or R&B sound, until Scott Alvin of The Majors joined The Scott Brothers in 1963.Instead of pointing to the future,The Majors' records of '52 and '53 were more like The Ravens' records of an earlier genre while their gospel brothers, The Four Fellows, were successful in the vanguard days of Rock 'n' Roll in 1955.Beckum's recording career with The Majors was never really profitable.He earned $25.00 for his Derby records that included lead singing and writing.Beckum's activity on the R&B scene became dormant until his cousin, a bright young lead singer named Willie Winfield, invited him to join The Harptones in 1955.[10]

[1] Interview with Clyde McPhatter,December 25,1971.

[2] Interview with Roland Martinez,April 29,1972.

[3] Clyde McPhatter interviewed by Marcia Vance,April 1972.

[4] It is not sure that The Dominoes and Checkers were meant to be rivals.They recorded for companion labels, Federal-King, used the same harmony, and virtually the same name. King may have been trying to capitalize on the sound and popularity of The Dominoes by signing a similar act.The Checkers copied The Dominoes to the tee;utilizing the church type harmony,the emotional high tenor leads of Little David Baughn who sounded just like Clyde McPhatter, the floating tenor background,the rocking gospel rejoicing on fast tunes,and Bill Brown's bass leads on "The White Cliffs Of Dover" and "Don't Stop Dan". The latter was the perfect sequel to "Sixty Minute Man".

[5] Billboard,April 12,1952, page 36 and July 19,1952,page77.

[6] McPhatter,December 25,1971.

[7] Sal Passantino,"For Collectors Only",Bim Bam Boom,Vol.I, No.5,May 1972,page 41.

[8] Nolan Strong is a cousin of Barrett Strong,whose recording of "Money" (Anna) was a hit in 1960.Barrett Strong also produced and wrote for Motown in the sixties and seventies.

[9] Interview with Nolan Strong,November 20,1971.

[10] Interview with Jimmy Beckum,September 21,1971.

Chapter 4

"Life Is But A Dream"- The 115th Street

Tin Can Band Makes It To The Apollo

It is a lonely Harlem night in early 1954 as you are out strolling along 119th Street. You have just broken up with your girlfriend and as you pass the African-Methodist-Episcopal Emanuel Church on West 119th Street, you hear a sad melody. The melody seems to console you and at the same time reminds you of your world that has seemingly ended. The sound is forlorn; it is mellow; and it is sad. It appears to be emanating from the A. M. E. Emanuel Church because you hear an organ; it is church music; it is gospel; it has a touch of the blues and; like your heart, it beats slowly. The organ finishes its introduction and the lead singer, in a rich, somber, breathy, broken tenor voice begins to share his sympathy with you.

You are of course not listening to a gospel program from the A. M. E. Church but rather you have just passed a rehearsal at the home of Raoul J. Cita, writer, organizer, mentor of one of the most respected ballad singing quintets ever to be born on the streets of New York City, The Harptones. The Harptones have just finished listening to the flip side of their first release, "Sunday Kind Of Love"/ "I'll Never Tell" which at the time was a highly respected blues ballad in black communities.

The Harptones began not on a street corner but in a school yard. Many neighborhood youngsters would gather in the school yard of the Wadley Junior High School on 115th Street between 7th and 8th Avenues. The Wadley schoolyard is not a suburban schoolyard; thirty feet long by approximately fifteen feet wide, shrouded by dark red brick walls and steel wire protected windows. Poorly lit at night it might have held The Channels, Five Crowns and Harptones all rehearsing at once. Next door to the school today is a contemporary type city schoolyard complete with basketball courts and high steel wire fences; a schoolyard which replaced a line of Harlem brownstones. In the old days there would be the usual stickball games, block parties and concerts out of which many of the groups of the fifties were formed. In 1951 three life long friends got together and started what was to become a neighborhood rage for the calypso sound. Bill Dempsey who lived in that old line of tenements got together with his pals across the street,Curtis Cherebin and Fred Taylor,and started making music by playing on tin cans.They put together a song called "Pork Chop on the Wall", played it in that diminutive schoolyard and performed it at neighborhood block parties.

The 115th Street Tin Can Band was so well received that the group decided they could expand on their talents, and venture off the block perhaps even to amateur night at The Apollo. Freddy, Dempsey,and Curt began harmonizing on the corners of 115th Street and 7th and 8th Avenues where they met Eugene "Sonny" Cooke and a second cat unknown except for his street nickname,"Skillum".The guys knew they had something as they were into singing and just having a good time while other street corner gangs in such far away places as Brooklyn were still archaic in relishing the excitement from gang wars and hot cars.[1]As they gathered material to sing, they named themselves The Skylarks. Soon after,Freddy allegedly penned a love ballad, "My Dear Dearest Darling". Ironically the song was later to become the first hit recording for The Five Willows who were back East on Lenox Avenue between 114th and 115th Streets.Street songs had a habit, in those early days,of exchanging hands rapidly.

In 1951 The Skylarks entered an amateur night contest at The Apollo.People on the block were astir with excitement. Demp,Freddy,Curt,"Sonny",and "Skillum" were going to make it on the big stage.When they got to the backstage entrance of The Apollo on 126th Street,they were apprehensive.Once inside, their anticipation turned to horror. "Sonny" sang a song and Freddy's young tenor voice squeaked through part of "My Dear Dearest Darling".Apollo patrons who are reportedly the toughest audience in the country,lustily booed The Skylarks. The Skylark's performance of "My Dear Dearest Darling" was atrocious.Midway through the song,the MC ordered them to leave the stage.The feeling of failure captured everyone. When they left the theatre, they received catcalls.Dempsey took the 7th Avenue route home that night to avoid embarrassment on 8th Avenue.But as he turned the corner at 115th Street, he could see the gauntlet already perched atop the short iron schoolyard fence.It was too late to turn back and hide. He could hear: "Hey man, I saw you get booed off the stage.You stunk!"It took forever to reach that old brownstone. Tears were shed at each additionally unsympathetic,"I heard you flopped". Once they were all inside, only an understanding father's consolation soothed the young Skylarks' broken hearts.The Skylarks finished last on that Summer Wednesday night in 1951.The winning act was a black quartet called The Diamonds: Daniel Stevens (bass), Myles Hardy(first tenor),Harold "Sonny" Wright(lead),and Ernest Ford (second tenor - guitarist), who received a recording contract with Atlantic Records.Later,Wright joined The Regals who became Sonny Til's new Orioles in 1956 and then Wright formed The Metronomes in 1957.[2]Little did The Skylarks know that night that they would eventually attain greater prominence.

The first stepping stone in any group's career was the all important first demo record. The Skylarks did not ignore this unwritten rule for street corner groups.However, like their appearance at The Apollo,their first demo record was a total disaster.They started hanging out at a record store on 116th Street between Lenox and Fifth Avenues where many other groups had hung out. The Singing Wanderers,who by 1952 had recorded for the Decca label,were regulars in the store.Then the owner of another store on 124th and Lenox wanted The Skylarks to cut a demo of a song he had.The Skylarks refused and insisted on making the dub of Freddy's "My Dear Dearest Darling".The store owner's song,"Crying In The Chapel"was later successfully recorded by The Orioles."My Dear Dearest Darling" in a trail unable to trace,ended up in the hands of The Five Willows who recorded the song a year later for the Allen record label.To this very day,Freddy Taylor will swear that it is his song,as will Tony Middleton who sang lead for The Willows.

Singing on the street corner was more than just an avocation for groups of the fifties,it was a life style.It seemed that group members were always joining,leaving and rejoining.After the demo record fiasco, The Skylarks began this process of expansion and disintegration too.They first met up with a piano player/song writer extraordinaire named Raoul J.Cita,who immediately added his original uptempo jump ditty, "Fine Little Girl" to their street corner repertoire. Cita had been a member of a club that promoted dances.At the time he was looking for someone to sing at a dance sponsored by his social club at Bowman's(155th Street and St. Nicholas Place).His sister called his attention to the group led by Dempsey so that he could polish up their ragged harmony for the gig at Bowman's.The Skylarks continued their nightly rendezvous on the corner and their brief encounters at local dance halls where "Fine Little Girl" was always a groove.

41

Curtis' lead and the group's accompanying chatter on the song seemed to reaffirm the pure street corner status of The Skylarks:

    Gotta fine little girl,   ) 2 X
    Best lookin' girl in town,)

    She's got one trouble,   ) 2 X
    She loves to fool around.)

    How fine she'd be   ) 2 X
    If she would stay on the square)

    I'd keep tellin' her,   ) 2 X
    But she don't seem to care.)

    Walkin' all around as sad as I can be   )2 X
    Tryin' to find somebody who will be true to me.[3])

Attrition began to have an effect on the group. "Sonny" Cooke left the group altogether. Cita stopped working with The Skylarks in 1952 until they reformed as The Harps in 1953. Johnny Brown of the "Laugh-In" television show joined occasionally to vocalize on the corner. Curtis became friends with a young Billy Brown and taught him some of the bass parts he was accustomed to singing. Shortly thereafter, Curtis' mother insisted that he get off the street and into school where he belonged. Fortunately for The Harptones, Curt's tutelage paid off in that Billy became the group's bass singer. As he grew older, Fred Taylor's voice became deeper and he developed a reputation in the trade as a "gypsy singer". He had tryouts and stints with The Five Crowns on 115th Street, The Carnations who were uptown, The Orioles and Carnation Charley's groups: The Quintones and Drifters. Fred never lost his loyalty to The Skylarks. His friendships in the neighborhood simply carried him from group to group. Street corner groups were merely an outward manifestation of the interlocking personal relationships that were assumed and broken in school, on the stoop, in the schoolyard, or even in those choose-up stick ball games. On a hot Spring day in 1959, Fred was offered a chance by Ben E. King to join the new Drifters as a bass. By 1959, Fred Taylor who had found street corner singing easy compared to what he emulated in Sinatra, Cole, and Ella Fitzgerald, had had enough of groups, records and corner harmonizing.

The Skylarks/Harptones became the classic example of the early New York street corner singing groups whose members and tunes were borrowed and exchanged and whose mellow harmonizing could be heard up and down Lenox,7th and 8th Avenues.Yet they were also a paradox.They were not necessarily a neighborhood group but yet a group with two nucleii, one uptown and the other downtown.As singers from the two neighborhoods merged in 1953,the original Harptones as they recorded included Willie Winfield(lead tenor), who was in The Apollo audience on the night of The Skylarks' flop, Nicky Clark(second lead and first tenor),Bill Dempsey(second tenor),Bill Brown(bass), Bill "Dicey" Galloway(baritone) and Raoul J.Cita on piano and occasionally doubling as baritone or tenor. A long series of events followed including more gigs at "Apollo Amateur Night" and "Spotlight On Harlem." Here is how it happened.

Before coming to New York City in 1953,Willie Winfield lived in Norfolk, Virginia, near his cousin Dickie Smith, who at that time was lead singer of The Five Keys(Newport News, Virginia),on such standards as "Ghost Of A Chance", "White Cliffs Of Dover", and "When You're Gone".Most collectors believe that these recordings were never released. However,both Willie Winfield and Rudy West believe that they were released only locally in Virginia.The Keys' influence on Willie was so strong,that The Harptones used "Glory Of Love", a Keys' standard as a back-stage warm-up.When things didn't work out with The Keys, Willie moved to New York City and joined a group called The Harps (The Winfield Brothers). Singing as The Harps under the Manhattan Bridge at Monroe Street on New York's lower East Side were Willie,his brothers Clyde and Jimmy Winfield,"Dicey" Galloway and Johnny Bronson.

In early 1953,while The Skylarks were struggling in Harlem,"Dicey" went looking for a piano player and was lucky enough to find a willing Cita and Dempsey.On the same corners of 115th and 7th and 8th was another group, managed by Lover Patterson, which held close ties to The Skylarks from the schoolyard days. The Five Crowns included Wilbur "Younkie" Paul, Dock Green, and the brothers Clark: James "Poppa" Clark,·John "Big John" Clark and Claudie "Little Nicky" Clark.[4]As friendships were broken,new ones made and greetings received from the Selective Service System,"Dicey" and Willie joined Cita, Dempsey and Curtis.They worked on "Sunday Kind Of Love" and Cita gave them "My Memories Of You," the first of a few songs that he had simply written as a hobby.

Soon Billy Brown replaced Curtis as the group's bass, Nick Clark was added as a second lead and tenor and the name Skylarks was dropped in favor of The Harps' tag because of the smooth, beautiful, ballad type harmonizing that the group evoked. After appearing at local gigs in Manhattan, Brooklyn and New Jersey including "Spotlight On Harlem", a New York television show, (their very first gig was at The Picadilly Club in New Jersey where six Harps collectively earned the grand total of one hundred dollars for two nights work), The Harps felt that they were ready for another shot at The Apollo.[5] The Harps did return to "Apollo Amateur Night" with Cita (actually only Dempsey was returning) and captured the hearts of the world's toughest audience with their blues oriented and magically sentimental version of "Sunday Kind Of Love". This time The Harps were on their way as they were met by a representative from MGM records who was in The Apollo audience. By accident they met Leo Rogers of Bruce records as they were singing in the hallway of the building where they were to meet the MGM man. Rogers, Morty Craft and Monte Bruce, the tri-owners of Bruce records signed them to a contract. Realizing that another group called The Harps recorded for Savoy records in Newark, New Jersey, Monte asked Cita to change the name of the group. Ironically the other group was Little David (Baughn) and The Harps who hailed from Newport News, Virginia. Cita suggested the name be changed to Harptones, Bruce filed papers of incorporation for the new name and The Harptones were born.

Vocal groups who appeared on the R&B recording scene as late as 1954 were influenced vocally by the earlier more innovative groups. The Harptones were no exception. The most profound influence on The Harptones was held by The Five Keys. In addition to the geographic proximity of The Keys and Willie Winfield, there were several Keys' standards that were used as models for the early Harptones' rehearsals. Harptone harmonies were patterned after "Glory Of Love" "How Long", and "When You're Gone". A dance routine for stage shows was based on "Hucklebuck with Jimmy", a Keys' uptempo number that was led by Maryland Pierce. Although The Harptones did in fact have a style all their own, Willie's voice could be likened to Rudy West's, Nicky's to Dickie Smith's and "Dicey's" to Maryland Pierce'.

There were also other groups whom The Harptones admired. An early Baltimore group, The Swallows was one of them. The Swallows were one of the pioneer bird groups who set many R&B standards to which the young Harptones aspired. Led by

Herman "Junior" Denby and Eddie Rich along with guitarist "Money", Earl Hurley, and Dee Ernie Bailey, The Swallows burned up the R&B circuit in the early fifties with such ren- ditions as "Beside You","Tell Me Why",and"Since You've Been Away".The smooth harmonies of The Swallows influenced The Harptones and in turn The Swallows' style of the sentimental lead and velvet haunting harmony had been indicative of the early fifties style previously established by The Ray-o-Vacs from the Sharp and Decca labels and the West coast's Johnny Moore's Three Blazers who featured the crooning piano player, Charles Brown. Brown's style of warbling was very similar to Denby's. In their formative years, The Harptones paid close attention to a New York group called The Larks.Led by the sweetest sounding lead around,Eugene Mumford along with Allen Bunn, David McNiel, Therman Ruth,and Ray Barnes,The Larks were also featured at The Apollo and on "Spotlight On Harlem".The Larks were the first group to use the bass singer in the style that was made popular by The Moonglows on "Sin- cerely" and "Most of All", and then later by thousands of groups."In My Lonely Room" featured the "doe-doe-doe"type of bassing which seemed to be taking the place of a bass fiddle in its absence on the street corner. The Larks had other standard hits for Apollo including "Stolen Love","I Live True To You", "Eyesight to the Blind" and the forever beautiful, "My Reverie".

When it came time to record, The Harptones embarked on a dual career,one as the bread and butter artists for the Bruce label and another as a studio backup group for Bunny Paul on Essex,Dickie Smith on Bruce,Ruthie McFadden on Old Town, Carol Blades on Gee, The Woodside Sisters on RCA and Herb Lance on Bruce.The Harptones began their career at Bruce records where fourteen sides were recorded,thirteen of which were released while the group's contract was active. They began the Bruce label with the Frank Sinatra standard,"Sun- day Kind Of Love", consequently competing in R&B circles a- gainst another group, Bobby Hall and The Kings (Robert J. Hall, Gilbert Wilkes,Leon Smith, John L.Rush,Richard Hol- comb, and Delphus Holcomb-Harlem,Jax,RCA,Gotham and Jalo) who were from Baltimore. The Harptones' version sold well in the New York metropolitan area and in Cleveland(due to Alan Freed's influence in the two areas) while The Kings' rendition did well in the Baltimore,Washington and southern districts.Actually,when The Harptones went out gigging on "Sunday",they were told about The Kings' version to their surprise and that the public preferred their flip side,"I'll

Never Tell".Regardless of the peoples' acceptance of "I'll Never Tell","Sunday Kind Of Love" became the R&B standard for other groups to follow usually in an uptempo vein,i.e. -The Del Vikings,Sentimentals,and Timetones.The song that permanently established the original style of The Harptones was Cita's original composition,written,rehearsed,practiced and polished in that West 119th Street basement,"My Memories Of You".Cita actually had "My Memories Of You" and the most famous Harptones' jam of all-"Life Is But A Dream"-at the same time;but "Life Is But A Dream" was not released until 1955 when the recording company and some of the members of the group had changed.The paraphrase, "Life could be a dream" could be heard in "Sh-boom",a 1954 hit by The Chords, later recorded by The Crew Cuts.

Cita also wrote "It Was Just For Laughs" which he would like to forget;but he cannot forget about the Bruce label's fourth release,"I Depended On You", which was beautifully sung by second lead, Nick Clark.Nick was a rare artist who on this number as well as others was able to maintain beautiful and complete control from natural voice to falsetto and back to natural. He had learned his lessons well from the early days with The Five Crowns on 115th Street.Perhaps that is why he was picked to sing the high ranging tenor lead in" I Depended On You" when Willie missed rehearsal one night. When Willie returned,the boys had picked out a note so high that Willie couldn't make it;Nicky was chosen and even had to switch notes in the channel of the song with Willie.When the group appeared in person without Nick,requests for "I Depended On You" had to be squashed.The song just could not be done without Nick Clark.

Another Rhythm and Blues group standard established by The Harptones was "Since I Fell For You".A classic in its own right, The Harptones were the first R&B group to make it a hit thanks to the suggestion of Buddy and Ella Johnson whom they met while on a bill together at The Apollo in 1954. Even today purists compare Willie's soulful interpretation of the Buddy Johnson tune with Lenny Welch's smash reading of 1963.Nothing,however,nothing,can best that extra smooth closed mouth high falsetto harmony on a record that was one of Alan Freed's first hits when he came to New York City in the Fall of 1954.Before they recorded for Bruce,The Harptones used to rehearse a song they nick-named "school girl" which was about a chick so out of sight that even a school education couldn't teach her young man about what it was like to love her."Loving A Girl Like You" was sung in the classic five part Harptone harmony;the soft tenor lead,the smooth blend of second tenor and baritone,the high falsetto of the first tenor,the redoubtable bass and the mournfully heavy affirmation of the R&B piano chords.An echo chamber effect was later added but this beautiful record, one of the first about a teenage love affair in school, an almost anti-school critique, was never released during the contract between the group and the owners of Bruce.Only in 1963,well after the contract had expired,was the master released on a "collectors series",a collectors series that included only one release pressed and printed without music publishing credentials. Needless to say The Harptones did not receive one penny for this just as they have not received much for any so-called collectors re-issues and repressings that have been released since The Harptones stopped actively recording in 1964.Call it expiration of the statute of limitations, expiration of contract, question of legal ownership or what have you,but how can an artist who created something not be compensated when his work is sold over and over again?The Harptones did receive some compensation for their performance of the R.J. Cita creation when they backed up Ruth McFadden on the answer song,"Schoolboy" for Hy Weiss' Old Town label.After their last recording for Bruce,Ivory Joe Hunter's "I Almost Lost My Mind", Leo Rogers brought them to Hy Weiss who started the Paradise label as a favor to Rogers.[6]The Harptones' exit from Bruce just about marked the demise of this early R&B independent.The Harptones were by far the cream of the crop of artists who recorded for the company whose offices were located at 1650 Broadway in Manhattan.Dickie Smith,The Mastertones, The Jumping Jacks,Joe Panama,Herb Lance and Don Gardner's Sonotones with Jimmy Smith made up the rest of the Bruce recording stable.Perhaps if the owners of Bruce had not been so cautious and had properly exploited the talents and reputation of Raoul Cita as organizer and arranger for many groups in the community,Bruce might have been an early predecessor of the Motown complex.The Hearts,a girls group which at one time featured Justine "Baby" Washington and Rex Garvin passed through Cita's door and out Bruce's before they got that "great big ol' lump o' sugar" together on "Lonely Nights" for Baton records. In fact they had even recorded a master of the song for Bruce.The Valentines when they were known as The Dreamers before Richard Barrett's entrance,rehearsed a song, "For You" in Cita's basement. Later, when Richard joined, "Summer Love" was rehearsed by Cita before the group went to Old Town.[7] Eddie Cooley and The Dimples ecorded "Priscilla" for Royal Roost and an unrecorded group called The Quintones featuring "Carnation" Char-Hughes (Drifters) on "Over the Rainbow" fell from the sp of Bruce in a similar fate.

There have always been very few fifties R&B groups whose personnel remained forever intact as one entity either on record or in personal appearance. A vocal quintet might have five singing members but they were drawn from the corner, from the community and later when the group was professionally experienced, from the family of young people who were trying to survive and make a living while singing, recording and performing one-nighters. The Harptones were no exception to this general rule. From the time they first changed labels until their resurgence in 1971, The Harptones endured a series of personnel changes and substitutions.

In 1954 when "Dicey" was drafted, the soulful voice of Jimmy Beckum was added. "Dicey" returned to The Harptones for a brief stint on the Rama and Gee sides and then drifted to The Five Satins for a while in 1956 and 1957. Bill Galloway never returned again when The Harptones rebounded in 1961 and 1970 even though he was always part of the Harptone family.

The multi-faceted talents of Jim Beckum were added in 1954 as the group was looking for a soloist who could belt out those rockers that appealed so much to the audiences at The Apollo. A relative of Willie, Jimmy first recorded with the group on "Life Is But A Dream" after joining with good credentials. He had led The Majors on their very first recording, "Laughing On The Outside" which was later cut by The Harptones in 1959. The Majors' version was in an earlier type, simpler, more fundamental R&B style. The evolution of R&B singing and recording can be heard by comparing the two records. Jim also wrote the flip side, "Come On Up To My Room", and some other songs that have never been released; "That's What The Angels Said" (Rama), "You're Gonna Need Me Someday" (Paradise) and "I Kiss That Rose". In 1971 he replaced Curtis as the teller of fortune of the street corner man's lament on "Fine Little Girl".

No replacement was actually ever found for Billy Brown after his untimely death in 1956. It was a sad day for The Harptones and their fans in 1956 when Alan Freed announced the tragedy over radio station WINS. Bobby Jay (Robert Jeffers), today a radio personality with WWRL in New York City, but then a resident of 118th Street and later a member of The Laddins from the same block, said that Brown's funeral was one of the biggest he had ever witnessed in Harlem. He recalled seeing young girls crying as the funeral proce: passed 118th Street that day.

Later The Harptones did re-employ the services of Fr Taylor when Jimmy was sick and a girl, Harriet "Toni" Willi as a fill-in for Dempsey while he attended to his canc stricken father in 1956. "Toni was the foxiest chick tha all the groups had,even putting Zola Taylor of The Platters to shame," according to Demp.Toni's voice including two other Joytones (Vicki Burgess and Lynn Daniels) can be heard on "That's The Way It Goes" (Rama).These young ladies were a part of The Royale Cita Chorus,a blend of three of Cita's groups who backed up Willie Winfield,The Harptones,The Lyrics and The Joytones. "I Understand" (Gee)was recorded by The Royale Cita Chorus,a group that contained twelve Cita-trained voices: Willie Winfield, Nick Clark,Bill Dempsey, Bill Galloway and Jimmy Beckum of The Harptones,Vicki Burgess,Lynn Daniels and Margaret Moore of The Joytones, and Curtis Cherebin,Willie Boddie, Ronald "Tweetie" Ellis and an unnamed Barbara of The Lyrics.

In 1956, when "What Is Your Decision" was recorded for Leo Rogers' Andrea label,the session included Willie, Dempsey, Jimmy, and Bobby Spencer whom Cita has tagged as one of the finest harmony and lead singers around.Spencer also gave his services to The Velvetones (N.Y.C.),The Crickets, Chords,Cadillacs,Harold Winley's 1971 edition of The Clovers and today's revived Cadillacs.Curtis Cherebin made sporadic appearances with the group and did not regain full status until 1958 when he joined Willie,Dempsey,Harriet and Milton Love from The Solitaires.

As 1955 rolled around,The Harptones began to stay away from the "fine little girl on the square" on 115th and Lenox as the lyrics imply and were brought by Leo Rogers to Paradise or "paradise" depending on your point of view,to record what has become a Rock 'n' Roll standard,"Life Is But A Dream" and the follow up "My Success (It All Depends on You)".While they were at Paradise/Old Town,the group had also prepared "with harmony going down in seconds" according to Cita,the tightest rendition of "Please Kiss This Letter".This song was never recorded by The Harptones.They soon left Paradise/ Old Town to record for Roulette (Rama/Gee) as they felt that their records were being poorly promoted.The beautiful ballad, "Please Kiss This Letter" was eventually recorded by Herman Dunham and The Solitaires as a flip side on the million seller, "Walkin' Along".

The technical and professional pinnacle for The Harptones

was reached in the next period of their recording career. They were gigging for Alan Freed at The Brooklyn Paramount and Tommy Smalls at The Apollo and were recording songs that have had an everlasting sentimental value to their fans; "Three Wishes", "The Masquerade Is Over";the meaningful reminiscence of "Sunday Kind Of Love","On Sunday Afternoon" ; and the old classic,"The Shrine Of St. Cecelia" which was borrowed,but not intentionally,from the Royals' 1952 rendition.Of all the Rama and Gee cuts,if not all The Harptones recordings,their personal favorite, and definitely Raoul Cita's personal love is a song he meticulously wrote,"That's The Way It Goes".He planned the harmony for each and every voice on the record including all The Harptones and the accompanying Royale Cita Chorus. This ballad is still in The Harptones' repertoire today as a show stopping acappella number that has received countless standing ovations.This is the only Harptone song where the harmony notes were not improvised by the group members after learning the melody.All five harmony parts were intricately written by Cita creating this artistic classic.

A Harptones' personal appearance in the fifties was a sight to behold.You might have seen them at their first big time appearance for Freed in the Winter of 1954 at The Jersey City Armory or at any of the other emporiums on the R&B circuit;The Apollo and Rockland Palace in New York,The Mosque Theatre in Newark,The Howard in Washington,The State Theatre in Hartford,The Royal in Baltimore or The Club Copa in Pittsburgh.If they were not entertaining at a theatre or night club,then The Harptones were involved in those proverbial "battles of the groups" at community centers,armories and the like; i.e., in a Harlem C.C. against The Channels, or in Eagle Hall (New Haven) against The Nutmegs.You may have seen them appear in their interchangeable brown formals and cream colored wool suits which they bought at Reed's on 125th Street next door to The Apollo. If you were really lucky, you might have caught them in bermuda shorts at one of Freed's shows, as Freed never let them wear shorts again.You would have left any one of these experiences with a lasting impression,not so much from their melodic harmonizing on ballads, but rather from their acrobatic performances on fast tunes. A typical evening at The Apollo in 1956, when they appeared with Tommy Smalls,The Heartbeats,Bo Diddley,Bill Doggett, The Flamingos and Etta James,or in 1957 when they headlined with Hal Jackson,Annie Laurie and The Federals,would have demonstrated their reputation as one of the "baddest dancing

groups ever to grace the world famous stage" according to
Al Grannum (WLIB-WBLS-NYC) who was in the audience often.
  "Ou Wee Baby" usually kicked a show off.If you were un-
fortunate to get to one particularly early show,you may have
missed Willie.One day Nicky and"Dicey" took his place as Willie
was so late he showed up with his stage uniform over his pa-
jamas.The Five Keys' "Hucklebuck with Jimmy" or Cita's"Fine
Little Girl" was usually the finale.All of The Harptones had
those exciting quick steps,highlighted by Willie's hop step
which he learned patiently from George Nelson of The Orioles.
In the break of " Hucklebuck with Jimmy", Billy Brown or
Dempsey would ride on Willie's back to the delight of the
audience.On "Fine Little Girl", in a routine that has never
been seen again,"Dicey" or Billy would appear to be levitat-
ing while doing splits as Demp would be kicking at one of
them.No dance routine ever had more precisely executed split-
second synchronization. One mistake, and "Dicey" or Billy
would have been kicked in the face.And if this wasn't enough,
Cita would be putting on another show at stage right as he
played the piano while sitting on the floor. Apollo audiences loved every minute of it.When an Apollo audience has
loved you, anyone will love you.
  There was about a year and a half lay-off before The Harptones returned to Morty Craft and recorded six commercial
sides,the greatest of which was "No Greater Miracle", (Warwick). This time period, 1959-1960,could be considered as
the first era of rejuvenation for vocal group oldies. The
period was heralded in by WINS disc jockey, Bruce Morrow,
whose spinning of oldies and vocal group records gave impetus
to The Harptones' "Miracle". Other vocal groups whose new
recordings received a shot-in-the-arm at this time were The
Flamingos ("Nobody Loves Me Like You Do"),The Five Satins
("I'll Be Seeing You")and The Turbans ("Diamonds And Pearls".
A live stage review was presented at The Island Garden in West
Hempstead,Long Island,to promote these acts.After Warwick,
they moved over to Coed where they were guided by Billie Dawn
Smith,the successful arranger who had so much success with
The Crests on the same label and The Heartbeats and Avons
on Hull in the mid-fifties.By this time,The Harptones were
grasping for straws. Another try led them to "Buzzy" Willis
the former Solitaires' baritone at Cub(MGM).When this proved
unsuccessful,they answered Maxine Brown with "All In Your
Mind" on Companion in 1961.The Harptones drifted into obscurity after Cita produced the very beautiful "Sunset" in
1964 with Willie and Jimmy sharing the lead.Their last re-

cording actually was the "Little White Cloud That Cried" in 1965 which was a blues treatment of the Johnny Ray standard by the group without Willie Winfield. In an effort to find a new winning combination, they had changed their name to The Soothers for this recording on the Port label, a subsidiary of Jubilee. Cita also had a girls' group at this time called The Rubies who recorded "Zing Went The Strings Of My Heart" for Warren Troob's KT label. By this time it had become apparent that five part quintet singing had become passe and that The Harptones had simply run out of popularity as well as original material. They were finished until the Rock 'n' Roll revival of April 1970 at The Academy of Music Theatre in New York City. In fact had it not been for a strange quirk of fate, The Harptones never would have reformed. Just before the revival started in 1970, Willie was going to form a new group with the late Bill Brown (bass of The Dominoes and Checkers) and Cleveland Still (Dubs). As chance would have it, both Willie and Cleve rejoined their respective original groups.

Here is a group that was considered one of the greatest R&B vocal quintets ever to record with one of the best lead singers ever, including Tony Williams, Rudy West, Sonny Til and Nate Nelson. In 1971 they were considered the most exciting, most well-polished of all new old groups on the oldies circuit. These are not overstatements, yet why did the group not achieve the success later enjoyed by The Temptations, Chi-Lites or Dells? Personal tragedies, bad management, poor contracts and business practices, inexperience, plain old bad luck and most importantly, the lack of exposure outside the black cultural media were bad experiences that many fifties groups suffered. The Harptones were of course not excluded from this club of disappointed artists.

In 1956, Fritz Pollard produced the first Rhythm and Blues motion picture (before the Freed gems, "Rock Around The Clock", "Rock, Rock, Rock" and "Don't Knock The Rock"). The Harptones would like to forget this celluloid experience with d.j. Hal Jackson, gospel singer Linda Hopkins, The Wanderers and The Miller Sisters. The picture was an opportunity but it was poorly directed and financed. Cita's piano playing was not even in sinc with the sound track. A disaster!

Another sore point was that The Harptones felt that Bruce records, in the early days, could have exerted a greater effort in distribution and promotion, as their appearances were limited to the New York metropolitan area, Connecticut, New Jersey, and D. C.. They never had a chance to visit the

West coast even though their recordings had been heard there. There were some fifties groups who lost members in automobile accidents which occurred during those nocturnal struggles to get from one "one-nighter" to the next. The Harptones had their scares on one night odysseys to New Jersey and Ohio, but the bitter after-taste was really left by the run-down automobiles and shabby hotels that promised a monetary savings for family men such as "Dicey", Nick and Willie.

In the July 31, 1954 issue of Billboard, Bruce records ran an advertisement boasting: "everyone is whistling and singing to the greatest singing sensations in the nation."You would have to believe from this ad that The Harptones were going to make an awful lot of money due to their recording of "Why Should I Love You"/"Forever Mine".Perhaps you were right but for whom? Most recording contracts have a clause that prohibits the covering of a song by another company for a period of one, two or three months. A cover record, as it still exists today, is simply nothing more than another artist recording his version of a song originally recorded by a prior artist. However, during the 1950's this type of procedure took on peculiar characteristics. R&B records that had a potential hit value were recorded by black artists for small, not too wealthy, independent record companies whose resources for mass production, national promotion and "cleaning-up" the sound to make it palatable for white audiences were exceptionally limited. All a major company had to do was copy the lyrics and arrangement of an R&B hit, add an orchestra to accompany white sounding voices and it would have a nice natural hit with "white bread, mayonnaise, apple pie and all the trimmings". This experience happened to a myriad of 1950's R&B groups; The Flamingos, The Jewels, The Penguins, The Chords and The Moonglows to name only a few. Perhaps The Harptones were fortunate in that they were not so heavily and successfully covered as were The Spaniels and Moonglows. There were groups of good singers who picked up a song in a studio and could get national television exposure every day while The Spaniels could count their blessings if their street corner harmonies in Gary, Indiana could take them to The Regal Theatre in Chicago.

"The only really dirty thing that was done to us," according to Cita, was that "while we were doing twenty-two takes to record the whistling in "Why Should I Love You" for Bruce, The Four Lads whose offices were right down the hall in 1650 Broadway, released the same recording in one day as a flip side of "Skokian" which became a national hit." Naturally what juke box entrepreneur would want to put The Harptones' version on his list,when he could have the more popular Four Lads' rendition with an "A" side as a hit as well.That was the end of "Why Should I Love You" for The Harptones in juke boxes or anywhere until they themselves met up with Jack Paar in 1956.[8]

Later in 1956,as contestants on Arthur Godfrey's <u>Talent Scouts</u> television program,The Harptones performed "Why Should I Love You". In spite of finishing second and being subjected to ridicule by Godfrey's substitute host, Jack Paar,the group did manage to gain a few gigs from their appearance.The Harptones finished in a flat footed tie with the eventual winner. Cita claimed that if Godfrey had been present,two winners would be declared in the event of two contestants registering over 100+ on the applause meter. A disc jockey from Radio Station WLIB (New York) by the name of Evelyn rapped to Paar about The Flamingos,Cadillacs,and El Dorados.Paar made fun of all these names,too.[9]

The general subject of cover records was discussed, in part,in the following interview which took place on April 19, 1971.Present at the interview were Raoul Cita (RC),William Dempsey (WD), James Beckum (JB),Curtis Cherebin (CC), Willie Winfield (WW), and myself,(PG).

WD: Another fault that might have been against the company was that it usually had 30 days or 60 days or 3 months before a record could be covered.We didn't seem to get that much time.

PG: When records were being covered in the old days,was it just that anyone could go out and cover anyone else's record?

WW: That's the way it seemed to me.

JB: No,not really.The big companies would cover the small companies.The small companies had the artist and would put the record out.The big company because they had more facilities would put another record out. People like Georgia Gibbs and Pat Boone would cover the small artist and would get to the market first. By the time the small artist's record got to the total market, the big company and its artist had already covered and put the big artist out.That's why the big artist got more radio play and exposure than the small artist because the small company could not put out stuff as fast as the big company.

WD: That's why you were supposed to have so much time before; at least one month.

PG: There was supposed to have been a time limitation.I can remember when "Two Hearts, Two Kisses,"The Charms...

JB: They got the arrangements that nobody could copyright,

and they were stolen...

WD: When we recorded "Why Should I Love You", the Four Lads' offices were right down the hall. We put it out today, they had it out tomorrow.

JB: When Lavern had "Tweedlee Dee", before it could get to the market...

RC: ..no that record was a hit already. But Lavern said that Gibbs, her manager and arranger went to The Apollo to copy down her arrangement.

PG: "Tweedlee Dee" was a hit on Alan Freed's program in New York for perhaps two months, was selling well and being played in black neighborhoods.

JB: Right, but when Georgia Gibbs covered it, it became a hit nation wide.

WW: At that time the Rock'n'Roll and Pop fields were separate.

PG: That type of music, Rock'n'Roll, really didn't merge into the popular field until 1955. Just to give you one example, I can remember "Two Hearts, Two Kisses," as I mentioned before. It went very fast on Freed and then everybody, Frank Sinatra, Pat Boone, covered it.

WW: Same as Gene and Eunice who had "Ko Ko Mo", and Perry Como covered it. It was a hit in the Rock 'n' Roll field, then Perry Como did it and it was a hit in both fields.

PG: The Flamingos covered "Ko Ko Mo" too.

RC: And "I'll Be Home", Pat Boone covered it. But it's true though that a lot of these records were hits already.

WW: Even "Life Is But A Dream" was covered by Alan Dean.

RC: For Rama records.

WW: He did a beautiful job on it with strings.

WD: Any more questions before I start crying?

WW: We had a lot of records that were put on the shelf and were never released.

RC: Yeah, "Loving A Girl Like You".

JB: It all comes back to poor management, bootlegging -we just got caught up in one of those things.

PG: And you guys never got anything?

WW: Actually I don't think that much stealing was going on, but rather people were selling off, making money from each other and selling to the biggest company.

WD: Masters were traveling all over the place. We can't remember how many sides are still on the shelf because we would do four or five sides at a session; all with arrangements.

PG: Who would decide what sides should be released?

WD: The company.

PG: You had no say?

JB: And every quarter we would do four sides.After a year or so that's an awful lot of tunes that were unaccounted for.[10]

One addition to the subject of unreleased masters concerned the ten inch EP reportedly produced by Bruce. It was never released although a cover had been prepared.Had it been,it would have established precedent as being the first of any extended or long playing albums by a Rhythm and Blues vocal group.Other unreleased material included "I'll String Along With You", "That's What the Angels Said" written by Jimmy Beckum and "Pocketbook",an Otis Blackwell tune sung by Jimmy.

One very sad theme that is recurrent with many of the old groups is that many of them do not own copies of their own recordings.You would think that some momento would endure time,but there were usually overriding circumstances such as when Willie would take his last personal copy of a recording and place it in a local jukebox to plug The Harptones.When bankruptcy would come knocking on that local establishment's door,this small individual team effort would be nullified and along would go "Life Is But A Dream" and "No Greater Miracle".

In 1972,New York City's greatest group consisting of six beautiful people, Willie Winfield(lead),Bill Dempsey(first tenor), Jimmy Beckum (second tenor),Curtis Cherebin(baritone),Fred Taylor (bass) and Cita,had grown disgusted again and disbanded for good.Now The Harptones consist of Willie, Cita, Linda Champion and Lowe Murray (Fi-Tones).Demp,Curt, Fred and Hank Jernigan have their own group.

THE ANNOTATED HARPTONES DISCOGRAPHY

ESSEX I'll Never Tell/Honey Love
364 (with Bunny Paul)
Their first effort as a backup group in 1954. Recorded in New York City and distributed in Newark. Only Bunny was from Texas. Leo Rogers owned publishing rights to "I'll Never Tell" and arranged to have Harptones record it for his friend David Miller who owned Essex.

BRUCE A Sunday Kind Of Love/I'll Never Tell
101 A song that Willie brought to Cita when The Skylarks and Harptones first got together. "I'll Never Tell" once embarrassed Winfield when he had laryngitis at The Apollo. A patron upstairs in the notorious "buzzard's nest" yelled: "Hey baby,you can't sing." Willie just couldn't put out on the song after that.Al Caiola played guitar on this session.Recorded in November 1953, and released in January 1954.

102 My Memories Of You/It Was Just For Laughs
A Cita original recorded at the "accoustically perfect" Fulton Studios in New York. The reported Rapidtones version of "Memories" with Willie Winfield singing lead had been reputed to be a bootleg. Group never sang or recorded under name of Rapidtones.F/S sung by "Dicey" and written by Cita on subway one night after rehearsal.

104 I Depended On You/Mambo Boogie
Cita wrote "A" side which was recorded with only three musicians present: Don Gardner,Jimmy Smith and Al (last name unknown) on sax. All the other musicians had walked out, as Bruce was trying to record ten songs at once to avoid a January 1,1954 musicians' strike.That is why sound is empty.F/S is one of few occasions when four members of the group received writers' credit.

109 Why Should I Love You/Forever Mine
"Forever Mine" was originally sung very slowly as an old "grind 'em up".Group never dug the release,

as it was speeded up during the recording session. The "A" side was recorded with the intention of earning a gig at The Copacabana,the pinnacle beyond The Apollo.

113   Since I Fell For You/Oobidee-Oobidee Oo
Cita can be heard singing baritone on the "A" side. The recording studio cut the ending short without another take leaving out "You Took My Love"."Oobidee" was one of a series of fast songs likened after "Sh-boom".

123   Loving A Girl Like You/High Flyin' Baby
Recorded at Fulton Studios on same set as original "Memories". On this session, Don Gardner played drums,Jimmy Smith on organ.Because of the lyrics, the group tagged the "A" side "Schoolgirl", i.e., "I went to school, passed all my tests...., obey these rules,along with the rest... but I was not told 'bout loving a girl like you."[11]

128   I Almost Lost My Mind/Ou Wee Baby
The Ivory Joe Hunter standard was accompanied by two of the greatest studio musicians of the fifties era. Sam "The Man" Taylor played tenor horn with Mickey "Guitar" Baker (later of Mickey and Sylvia). Break was sung by Nicky. Willie always wanted to end song with falsetto:"This time she's gone for good--bye,bye baby,bye bye."

PARADISE
101   Life Is But A Dream/You Know You're Doing Me Wrong
Band was led by blind saxophonist,Sam Kimble and organ played by Roger "Ram" Ramirez. F/S is led by Jimmy on a rocker similar in background style and lead to "Fine Little Girl".

103   My Success (It All Depends On You)/I've Got A Notion
A good song that was neglected in the early days and today in revival period. Not pushed because of similar lyrics in a Georgia Gibbs song. "My Success" had to be added to change title.

ANDREA
100   What Is Your Decision/Gimme Some

Recorded with an electronic piano;a recording in-
novation at the time. Group consisted of Willie,
Demp,Jimmy,Bob Spencer and 3 Joytones;Vickie Burgess, Margaret Moore and Lynn Daniels. Harptones
dislike the ending of "Decision".Willie tried to
be cute by hitting an off-note-that's just how it
was released.

TIP TOP

401 My Memories Of You/High Flyin' Baby
The 1956 version of the classic was recorded on same
night as "What Is Your Decision", with same per-
sonnel.Leo Rogers probably owned Tip Top and sold
master to George Goldner (Gee) as it appeared in
"Teenage Party" LP.

RAMA

203 Three Wishes/That's The Way It Goes
"A" side introduction contains varied leads among
Willie, Nicky and"Dicey".

214 On Sunday Afternoon/The Masquerade Is Over
Two of the most beautiful recorded at Bell Sound
Studio in New York in 1957.

221 The Shrine Of St. Cecilia/Ou Wee Baby
A classic originally recorded in 1952 for R&B by
The Royals (Midnighters)with Henry Booth(lead) for
Federal. Cita knew little of the original even
though the arrangements were quite similar. Song
was popular when Skylarks were just beginning.Harp-
tones had planned it to be first release until Willie pointed record out on juke box to Cita while
they were singing on a gig in New Jersey.This is
the last record made by Billy Brown.

GEE

1045 Cry Like I Cried/So Good, So Fine, You're Mine
The first time they used horns on this verydifficult
to sing song.F/S is duet between Harriet and Willie,written by Cita while touring in South Carolina
in 1956.

Warwick

500 Laughing On The Outside/I Remember

When the group first returned to Morty Craft, they revived the old Jimmy Beckum and The Majors' tune, one of Cita's personal favorites. Recorded at the RKO studios on 106th Street in Manhattan. Willie, Demp, Nick, Curt, and three Joytones sang on the session.

512 Love Me Completely/Hep Teenager

551 No Greater Miracle/What Kind Of Fool
Still one of the most exciting songs to hear. Recorded at the newly equipped RCA Victor Studios on 22nd Street and Lexington Avenue in Manhattan in 1959. Harmony assisted by just two of the Joytones, Vickie Burgess and Lynn Daniels. Willie was taught part of the lead voicing by Wilbur "Younkie" Paul (Five Crowns) who led on the F/S.

COED
540 Rain Down Kisses/Answer Me My Love
Produced by Billy Dawn Smith, former lead of The Heralds (Herald), The Billy Dawn Quartet (Decatur) and The Four Dukes (Duke).

CUB
9097 Devil In Velvet/Your Love Is A Good Love
Produced by Winston "Buzzy" Willis, formerly of Solitaires, at MGM.

COMPANION
102 All In Your Mind/The Last Dance
Maxine Brown gave Willie the idea to answer her hit of 1960, "All In My Mind". The recording sounded just like Maxine Brown's original. F/S sung by the Bill Withers sound-a-like, Hank "Pompi" Jernigan.

103 What Will I Tell My Heart/Foolish Me
"Foolish Me" begins as a facsimile to "Sunday Kind of Love".

KT
201 Sunset/I Gotta Have Your Love
Their last recording as The Harptones in 1964. Written by the group's lawyer's son, Ted Troob and produced by Cita. Recorded on same session as Rubies'

"Zing, Went The Strings".

BRUCE
BEP-201 A Sunday Kind Of Love/Ou Wee Baby
Forever Mine/I Almost Lost My Mind

BEP-202 My Memories Of You/Mambo Boogie
I'll Never Tell/High Flyin' Baby

THE SOOTHERS

PORT
70041 I Believe in You/The Little White Cloud That Cried
The "A" side was an original Hank Jernigan and Bill
Dempsey James composition and production which Hank
led.The F/S was led in a moving blues/gospel style
by Nick Clark. Without Willie, The Soothers, who
changed their names from The Philharmonics, consisted of Hank, Demp , Nick, Curt, Fred,and Cita
with his piano.

BACK UP WORK FOR OTHER ARTISTS
BRUCE Dickie Smith
? When You're Gone/Hucklebuck With Jimmy
Recorded on same session as the first "Memories of
You".

? Herb Lance
Seems Like You Just Don't Have A Heart/?

OLD TOWN Ruth McFadden
1030 United We Stand/ School Boy
Cita did all kinds of work for her and Old Town,
all for nothing.Group backed her up on "Schoolboy"
which was same song as "Loving A Girl Like You",
("Schoolgirl").

GEE Carol Blades
1029 When Will I Know/What Did I Do Wrong
Carol was only 13 or 14 years of age when she sang
with The Harptones.

RCA Woodside Sisters
? So Soon/ ?

[1]By the late and mid fifties,the neighborhoods of Brooklyn (Bedford- Stuyvesant and The Fort Greene Projects)had given birth to a host of solid street corner groups. Many were closely associated with each other.There were The Five Chimes,The Caverliers Quartet, and The Fi-Tones.The Duponts, Chesters,Chips,Velours and Little Anthony and The Imperials were also closely tied.The Chips were a group born out of difficulties in the street.Formed on the Bedford-Stuyvesant corner of Clifton Place and Grand Avenue, The Chips (Sam Strain,Charles Johnson,Paul Fulton,Shedwick "Bubby' Lincoln and Nathaniel Epps) recorded "Rubber Biscuit",the incredible lunchroom chant from The Wiltwick Home For Boys.Earlier a school yard basketball team called The Dell-Vikings, had changed its name to The Mellowlarks to compete in local group battles against The Five Willows,Solitaires and Vocaleers. The Mellowlarks,including Clarence Quick, William Blakely and occasionally Joe Lopes, (the quitarist on "Whispering Bells") disbanded when military service called.Quick began a vocal Dell-Vikings in Pittsburgh where he was stationed with the Air Force.He was joined by Corinthian "Kripp" Johnson,Norman Wright,Don Jackson and Gus Backus.When the group made its famous "Come Go With Me" in a Pittsburgh basement, David Lerchey replaced Don Jackson.The famous singer, Chuck Jackson, was not an original Dell-Viking at this earliest date. The Dell-Vikings were a solid singing quintet whose reputation was built around the fact that they were one of the first integrated groups.Lead singer Norman Wright lost deserved recognition when Air Force duties forced him to miss a nationally televised Alan Freed gig in 1957. Gus Backus was later erroneously billed as the former lead singer of The Dell-Vikings.Interviews with Sam Strain,July 13, 1971 and William Blakely, October 31,1971.

[2]Letter to Bim Bam Boom by Harold "Sonny" Wright,interview conducted by T.Denehy.

[3]"Fine Little Girl",by R.J.Cita,unpublished.

[4]The Five Crowns fit into the pattern of other groups in that many of their members sang with other groups;i.e.-Dock Green also sang with The Five Willows,Crowns,Drifters and a revived Moonglows, "Poppa" Clark also with The Cadillacs and The Crowns and "Younkie" with The Harptones. The Five

Crowns also sang under the name of The Duvals.

[5]These gigs included Community Centers in Harlem and the Englewood,New Jersey Jewish Center (1954) where The Harptones battled with The Dreamers (Valentines).

[6]Interview with Hy Weiss, July 10, 1971.

[7]Interview with Ronnie Bright, formerly bass of Valentines, current bass of Coasters and studio backup voice for Roberta Flack ("Go Up Moses").

[8]Interview with The Harptones at rehearsal,April 19,1971.

[9]Ibid.

[10]Ibid.

[11]R.Cita,Bruce Records, 1954.

Chapter 5

The Lady In The Window

This time it is ten o'clock on a spring evening in 1955. While you sit in your apartment at 2406 Eighth Avenue in New York City, you can hear coming from beneath your window, the plaintive sounds of "window, window, window lady...". As you look to the playground below, silhouetted on a park bench are five young men whose voices sing to a pretty girl in a window above yours. The 129th Street projects in Harlem have become the rehearsal home for Charles "Buddy" Brooks, Earl Wade, Earl Carroll, Bobby Phillips and Laverne Drake. The loneliness of being without a woman had become a regular theme of street corner singing as The Cadillacs continued to sing about "Window Lady":

Window lady, sitting by your window,
Tell me what can be your name.
Pretty as a picture,
You're as pretty as a picture,
Sitting there behind your window frame.

Did your man run off and leave you?
All alone and now you're apart.
If I were yours, I'll never grieve you.
Let me come in,
Let me come in to your heart.

Window lady, sitting by your window,
Won't you take one chance with me?
I would take your sadness,
Turn it into gladness,
Window lady, let me in please do.
Oh window lady, I love you.

The group faded out with "blue, blue, blue, blue, blue" describing the lead singer's mood as Earl Carroll pleaded a falsetto "I love you". Part of this mid-fifties street scene is mere conjecture about the creation of the ballad,

"Window Lady". The Cadillacs, however, did rehearse their lyrics,harmonies,and routines at this spot after they had become professionals.The story of how they began as a vocal group goes back to the corners of 7th and 8th Avenues between 131st and 133rd Streets in Manhattan. Just as many young black singers were exercising their talents on park benches, in hallways, in project playgrounds,under bridge viaducts or in subway stations and arcades,these young men were developing a strong reputation for harmonizing on the street and wherever they appeared at local dances in schools, community centers,churches and block parties.The Carnations who could be recognized at public appearances by the flowers they wore in the lapels of their jackets,initially included Bobby Phillips,whose mother raised his near look-alike Earl Carroll,[1] Laverne Drake,and bass singer "Cub".[2]Gaining an early reputation as a tough group to battle,The Carnations used to go to the St. Mark's Church on 132nd Street for community dances to compete against other groups.It was at St. Mark's that The Carnations appeared with The Velvetones, another amateur group whose members ironically later replaced some of The Cadillacs when the latter's fame was diminishing[3]

In 1953,The Carnations decided to audition for the annual P.S. 43 talent show. The Carnations were a one of a kind act at this type of show;standing out among the Latin bands and interpretive dancers.It was at "43" that Lover Patterson, the organizer of The Five Crowns, discovered the group, suggesting that they should see Mrs. Esther Navarro,a secretary for Shaw Artists Booking Agency.Mrs.Navarro was also a good friend of Jerry Blaine at Jubilee Records.

When this break came,the guys decided on a little vocal re-organization.Bobby Phillips had been the baritone of The Carnations.He wanted to try something that had never been done before;he wanted to be a "little bass".(Phillips looked like he was about 5'4" tall.)The leader of the group,Earl Carroll,agreed that this might be something new and original.Being able to talk anybody into anything,Carroll's persuasiveness prompted this change for the group. "Cub" and two other guys who hung out with The Carnations (one was called "Butch" on the street),not wanting to leave the neighborhood security of the gigs at P.S. 43 and St. Mark's,rejected the innovation.Cub and his cohorts refused to go to Esther and try something so risky.Cub's Carnations remained a local attraction in the St. Nicholas Projects,continuing to gig at Rockland Palace and harmonize on playground benches in the projects.They eventually drifted into obscurity.Other groups used the same name for Derby and Savoy Records.

Patterson thought that the remaining nucleus of The Carnations needed some experience.When the group went to audition for Navarro,he suggested the addition of James "Poppa" Clark from The Five Crowns and Johnny "Gus" Willingham, also from 115th Street.Esther approved of the new members but she did not approve of the name,Carnations.She wanted the group to assume a strikingly unique name. In a story related by Bobby Thomas,lead singer of a group that recorded under the names Vibranaires and Vibes for"Luxie"Hanford's After Hours and Chariot labels respectively,Esther changed the name of The Carnations to what was to become the most exciting show stopping mark of excellence in the Rhythm and Blues field. [4]When Thomas brought his Vibranaires from Asbury Park,New Jersey,to sign a personal management contract with Esther Navarro and Jesse Powell,Josie's resident tenor saxophonist,the name Vibranaires also met with Esther's disapproval. Thinking the name was too long, Esther had The Vibranaires look through all kinds of bird and flower books. While this was going on,someone was looking out the window of her office and noticed a pink Cadillac."Hey look at the guy driving that pink caddy!", someone exclaimed. Another bystander remarked that "Cadillacs" wouldn't be a bad name for a group,as no one had ever dreamed of naming vocal groups after automobiles. Esther immediately liked the new name. She and Thomas wrote to Detroit for permission to use it. After permission was received from General Motors, Bobby and The Vibranaires were told to wait until the right time for their first release under her management.The boys were young,green and impatient.They pestered her day after day about recording to no avail. Within a month, Bobby Thomas heard the "Cadillacs" name used publicly as "I Wonder Why" was aired on the radio.The name "Cadillacs" had been created, but for The Carnations and not The Vibranaires. A new act was born and an old one, The Vibranaires was dead,discouraged, never to record again.

Josie Records,a subsidiary of Jubilee, carried two records by The Cadillacs ("I Wonder Why"/"Gloria" and "Wishing Well"/"I Want To Know About Love") until two of the original Cadillacs,Clark and Willingham were replaced by Earl Wade, lead singer of The Crystals and Opals and Charles "Buddy" Brooks respectively.[5]What followed was a mess of super bad recordings that set standards for rock-jump tunes as well as those "fish-grind" slow ballads.First lead singer,Earl Carroll, moaned that his girl had let him have "No Chance" and then Earl Wade left her as he went "Down The Road" to a chorus of never to be forgotten"Oh baby,whoop,moop,bow-wah-bop,be-doo-be,doo-be,doo-be-doo-be,doo-be's". In their most memorable rock ditty,Earl Carroll,whom everybody called "Speedy",but who preferred to be called Mr. Earl,allegedly penned a tune that was credited to Esther Navarro about how fast he was with "Takin' other folk's girls"."Speedoo" became the classic example of the happy R&B chant where the lead singer extolled his virtues as a lover,backed by a thumping bass voice,chattering vocal harmony ("Bah-bah-jib-a-dee"), a rocking tenor sax bridge and a melodic fade-away ending. This recording had everything;the bass beginning,followed by the vocal background, followed by the lead singer in a vocal pattern which was very similar to the African chant where vocal syncopation overlapped a leading melody or voice. "Speedoo" had a stop and go channel and a chattering harmony that faded away into the distance as "Speedoo" ahemmed his affirmation that he was so cool.The title of this song has always been "Speedoo". Listeners have just misinterpreted Carroll's reading of the lyric as "Speed-oh".Consequently, Carroll has been nicknamed "Speedo".

The connotation associated with the name Cadillacs was a fast,rocking,wild,cool one.But The Cadillacs could sing love ballads as well.Could they sing slow songs! When Wade and Brooks joined the group, the first ballad release was the gospel choir influenced "Sympathy". The full range of vocal harmony was so inspiring on this cut that it was possible to actually picture a choir singing at the St. Mark's Church.On another ballad,"Let Me Explain", the early influence of The Five Keys could be heard.Earl Wade's baritone lead was similar to The Keys' Maryland Pierce, when he sang "My Saddest Hour".The talking high tenor echo provided by Earl Carroll as he falsettoed "please let me explain" was a direct duplication of the same technique provided by The Keys' Rudy West as he echoed "....my saddest hour".The imitation of the older veteran groups by The Cadillacs was not unintentional.They had grown up on the streets of Harlem,aspiring to the achievements of The Orioles and The Moonglows.When Earl Carroll was sixteen,he personally dug The Moonglows' versions of "I Was Wrong","Good Rockin' Daddy" and "Lonely Christmas";records that were easily obtainable in the record shops of Harlem during the early fifties.It is no wonder that The Moonglows' trademark,the mellow sounding closed mouth blow harmony can be heard on The Cadillacs' most revered slow recording,the street song "Gloria".[6]Although it had traces of the earlier group styles,

"Gloria" is still today the epitome of the street corner ballad that most reflects what has become known as the "New York Sound".The song has been repeatedly copied by both black and white groups;The Passions,Channels,Vito and The Salutations.Other groups played word games with the title; notably The Five Thrills and Five Chances from as far away as Chicago.It should also be pointed out that it was the earlier groups whom The Cadillacs ironically passed and replaced in the show business limelight as their records became hits.

Esther Navarro was somewhat instrumental in this.She had been handling the booking arrangements as secretary for the Shaw Agency.When a customer would request The Five Keys or another act,she would offer The Cadillacs as an alternative. They were considered a more exciting attraction because of their choreography.At this time,the group was just beginning and in need of financial and professional assistance.They were working in a downtown place called "Snooky's".Without fancy outfits,the ragged Cadillacs worked nightly,polishing up their choreography and gaining valuable exposure on the bar and nightclub circuit.It has been rumored that The Cadillacs had nothing.To get advances,they supposedly signed a power of attorney,forwarding all of their earnings in return for a salary of seventy-five to one hundred-fifty dollars per week depending on the individual member. That is how it came to be later in their career that The Cadillacs were "looking good and doin' bad".[7]

While The Carnations had been evolving into The Cadillacs, their arch rivals in those St.Mark's battles,The Velvetones were undergoing some changes too. The Velvetones (usually Jimmy Bailey, Robert Spencer,Fred Barksdale and Champ Rollow) were known for their Eisenhower leather jackets.They wore this uniform because it was difficult to get four blue suits that all matched.No matter how hard one person tried to outfit the group,there was always one guy wearing a black suit. So The Velvetones, to make things easier,just adopted the dock worker appearance.Yet to this day,there is an old photography shop on 131st Street and 7th Avenue that once displayed a picture of The Velvetones.The picture showed those mismatched blue suits each with a "V" on the breast pocket.

Things started to happen for The Velvetones when Dave Mc-Phatter, Clyde's brother,who had been sporadically singing with The Velvetones,brought Fred Barksdale to the Masonic Lodge on 129th Street between 7th and Lenox Avenues to audition as a bass for The Dominoes.Bill"Sixty Minute Man"Brown,

The Dominoes' bass,had been planning to leave to join the offshoot Checkers. Fred proceeded to bass his way through "sixty minutes"amazing an incredulous Billy Ward.Ward asked Barksdale to join.The Dominoes were a hot group.Their pre-eminence petrified the young Barksdale.He was so frightened that he never returned for another rehearsal.

The Velvetones kept hanging out until they got word that Dean Barlow and The Crickets,a standard ballad quintet were breaking up. The guys idolized The Crickets' harmony;pure beauty in simplicity.They also dug The Crickets' uniforms which were not too simple;wide lapelled jackets,one button low; broad shoulders;"Mister B" rolled collars and big "V" tie knots.The Crickets had recorded"You're Mine" (MGM) before disbanding.As the record was breaking big, Joe Davis, (owner of Jay Dee Records) needed a group for personal appearances to back up Barlow."Ditto",a member of The Crickets, was leaving to join The Chords,the originators of "Sh-Boom". Spencer,Bailey and Barksdale joined Barlow and Harold Johnson to form the new Crickets.The new Crickets made some of the sweetest,mellowest recordings ever to come out of the Morrisania section of The Bronx where Barlow attended Morris High School. Their recordings of "Be Faithful", "Changing Partners", "Are You Looking For A Sweetheart", "For You I Have Eyes", and "I'm Going To Live My Life Alone" are R&B classics of closed mouth harmony.The beauty of The Crickets was tarnished by jealousies that existed between the old and new group;nearly resulting in a rumble on 168th Street and Boston Road in The Bronx.Eventually,Barlow went out on his own ("Forever","I'll String Along With You"-Beacon and"Two Flights Up"-Beltone in 1960); a decision that was not too popular with the rest of The Crickets. Johnson formed The Mellows, another Morrisania group with Lillian Leach,Carl Spencer and John Wilson.This marked the close of The Crickets' career.

Barksdale and Bailey then resumed their tours of The Rock-land Palace-Savoy Ballroom circuit,by forming another group called The New Yorkers Five with "Rocky"Smith,Shelly Dupont and Johnny Darren.They recorded a relatively unknown "Cha, Cha, Cha Baby" / "Gloria My Darling" for the Denise label owned by Mr. "Luxie" Hanford of Flaps' Record Shop on 125th and 7th. The New Yorkers Five hung out in Flaps' shop but nothing happened.There was no bread to push the record.It was then back to the leather jackets for Spencer,Bailey and Barksdale until The Cadillacs and Solitaires reformed in the middle and late fifties.[8]

One aspect of group theatrics that was never mastered by

The Crickets,Mellows,and Velvetones,was stage choreography. The Cadillacs were the stage masters of unparalleled choreography that was meticulously timed and arranged so each step would breathlessly excite any audience.When Esther Navarro was booking the quintet for Alan Freed's Christmas stage show at The Academy of Music Theatre in New York City in 1955, she hired Cholly Atkins of the famous Coles and Atkins dance team to teach the intricate dance routines to The Cadillacs. The group was also outfitted with the finest threads available;white jackets,red pants and those impressionable white shoes.

Certainly there had been predecessors, The Ravens and Orioles,who had danced on stage.None however,had perfected the art of stage step work as well as The Cadillacs.Their steps were not haphazard,they were synchronized;not crude but polished.These guys were so good on stage, that they actually detracted from the audio impression their records had made. All of this was due to the inimitable style and tutelage of Charles (Cholly Atkins) Atkinson.Today his lessons have been learned well by The Temptations and Bernie Wilson,vocal and choreographic leader of Harold Melvin and The Blue Notes.Atkins started at The Apollo,where his partner Charles "Honi" Coles became theatre manager,by training The Cadillacs and Sonny Til's neo-Orioles(formerly The Regals) in 1955.From then on,Atkins' school of choreography reads like a veritable who's who of Rock 'n' Roll;Frankie Lymon and The Teenagers,The Five Satins,Heartbeats,Coasters,Smokey Robinson and The Miracles when they recorded for Chess and End,Gladys Knight and The Pips when they recorded for Bobby Robinson's Fury label,and then finally on to Detroit and Motown in the mid sixties.[9]

The 1955 Alan Freed Christmas show was a dynamite gas but the final act,The Cadillacs was the show stopper.They sang their most famous uptempo tunes; "No Chance","Down The Road" and "Speedoo".Earl Carroll or Earl Wade and Bobby Phillips would sing on one mike and one of the Earls,Brooks and Verne on the other. Every note, every phrase, every sound had a corresponding visual choreographic movement;moving, strutting,sliding,turn arounds,splits and moving back together, bedazzled the audience.Many times the "little bass" Bobby, would hop back and forth between the lead and harmony mikes, often going down on one knee to riff his catchy bass phrases such as"...I'm goin' down the road".Every time he did that the audience would go wild and more crazy steps would ensue. The grand finale was indeed a sight to behold. The group

70

turned around, about faced again, hand clapped up to the mike in stride as "Speedo" did his thing with straw hat, cane and short-stepping strut. Bobby accompanied both the lead and background as he "bom-bom-bommed" back and forth. Splits and back-over-flips highlighted the tenor sax bridge by Sam "The Man" Taylor.Sheer noise rocked the theatre as Earl and The Cadillacs waved goodbye,fading behind the curtain while they were stepping out the closing fade-away to "Speedoo". It was this show stealing spectacle that established The Cadillacs' reputation as truly the vocal groups' "standard of excellence".

The Cadillacs set precedents that were soon imitated. The Valentines,The Five Satins,Otis Williams and The Charms and The Four Fellows all tried to outdo each other in fancy haberdashery.Heart monograms, multi-colored plaid jackets and white jackets with black shirts and white ties glittered these acts' appearances.The Cadillacs' success heralded in the era of the car name groups.A barrage of such names cluttered the Rhythm and Blues and Rock 'n' Roll market until 1961.The Belvederes, Montereys, Montclairs, El Dorados,V-Eights,Bonnevilles,Fiestas, Edsels, Starfires,Fleetwoods, The Imperials, The Lincolns, The Corvairs and even Speedo and The Impalas tried to capitalize on The Cadillacs' moniker. There were also songs entitled after cars. The Medallions did "Buick 59","Coupe De Ville Baby" and "59 Volvo";Young Jesse talked about his girl "Mary Lou" stealing the keys to his Cadillac car and the immortal Chuck Berry lyricized the fantasies and toils of Ford and Cadillac devotees in "Maybelline" and "You Can't Catch Me".Berry's most descriptive car song was however one of his least successful."No Money Down"talked about continental spares and wire chrome wheels.

As The Cadillacs were being flattered by their imitators, they also began to have difficulties.Continuity of sound and membership were two qualities that began to escape this likeable New York street corner group. Unlike The Temptations who have changed all but two members since their smash hit of "My Girl" in 1964,while growing musically and maintaining some recognizable sound, The Cadillacs began to disintegrate once members changed.

In early 1956,Jimmy Bailey from The Velvetones,Crickets, New Yorkers Five and Deep River Boys,replaced Laverne Drake. The next record,"Woe Is Me" signified a change in TheCadillacs' style.It became more jazz,blues and pop oriented and replaced the jump ditty and grind ballads of The Cadillacs' earlier R&B and Rock'n'Roll styles. This change which was financially not as rewarding as the "Speedoo"/ "Zoom" days endured through the more sophisticated "Betty My Love" and "The Girl I Love".Only "Shock-a-Doo" and "Sugar-Sugar" were attempts to regain the old days.Then disaster hit The Cadillacs.It is hard to tell the cause.Rumors persist that Mrs. Navarro and Jubilee's Jerry Blaine claimed counter-ownership of the group. The group split in half and two Cadillacs' quartets emerged in 1956-57.A return to the genuine street corner sound on "My Girl Friend"/"Broken Heart" was made by Bobby Spencer, Jim Bailey, Champ Rollow and Bill Lindsay. This group was pictured on The Cadillacs' first album in 1957. Earl Carroll was conspicuously absent from that cover. He then reformed The Original Cadillacs ("Lucy"/"Hurry Home") with Wade,Brooks and Phillips.

The rest of the history of The Cadillacs is such a hodge-podge conglomeration of singers from other groups that a detailed appendix has been added to this chapter.So many other groups, notably The Opals, Vocaltones and Solitaires, are intertwined with The Cadillacs,that their stories must not be overlooked.

After "Lucy",The Cadillacs embarked on a series of recordings that sounded as if they had learned the song and harmony patterns on the morning of the recording session. A change came in 1958 when the two groups merged reforming the full Cadillacs. "Speedo Is Back" signified the joining of forces between Wade-Carroll-Phillips and Spencer-Bailey. The Cadillacs' biggest selling record,"Peek-a-Boo",hit in the winter of 1958-59. Written by Jack Hammer,a member of the revival Platters,it marked the end of the famous Cadillacs' harmony and the beginning of an imitation Coasters' sound. "Holy Smoke", "Jay Walker", "Big Dan MacGoon" and "Please Mr. Johnson" were all comedy records, usually led by Bailey and Spencer. "Speedo" then refused to continue singing background. That is why "Romeo", a "Speedoo" facsimile had Spencer singing lead without Earl Carroll at all.

Another comeback and a fourth change in style occurred in 1960.Earl Carroll decided to reform the group again and hired Jesse Belvin's guitarist,the late Kirk Davis,Ronnie Bright from The Valentines,and Roland Martinez from The Vocaleers and Vocaltones.The end was now in sight."Tell Me Today" was rehearsed in Kirk Davis' room in The Cecil Hotel on 118th Street between 7th and 8th Avenues.By 1960,singing on the corner was no longer considered cool. "Tell Me Today",a real fine sound had failed.Then the revolving doors really began to turn.

Efforts were made several times to change the name back to The Original Cadillacs.Esther Navarro tried to publicize a former Penguin and Hollywood Flame,Ray Brewster as Bobby Ray.This attempt to achieve star status also failed."Speedo" was even matched up with a group called The Pearls (Howard Guyton, Derek Martin, et al.) to no avail.Members of different groups were brought in to recapture the solid harmony of the old days.Bobby Phillips returned as the group's bass, replacing Bright. At times, different record labels such as Mercury and Smash (a Mercury subsidiary) were used before Jubilee expired its catalog of Cadillacs' releases. The Smash and Mercury cuts were released before "I'll Never Let You Go" (Josie). Jubilee compounded the issue by continuing to release the "Wayward Wanderer" and long playing albums containing previously unreleased cuts by both the Carroll-Phillips and Spencer-Bailey groups.Esther tried to pull out all the stops on the Smash release in 1960, when "Speedo",Martinez and Brewster were teamed with the author of "Earth Angel",former Penguin,Curtis Williams and veteran bass singer,Irving Lee Gail, from The Pretenders,Miracles (Fury) and Vocaltones. Ray and "Speedo" sang a duet while an all-star cast supported them; Clyde Otis (production), Stan Applebaum (arrangements),Doc Severinsen(trumpet),and Perry Como's Ray Charles Singers. Result? Nothing! Within a year, "Speedo" left the group altogether to join Carl Gardner's Coasters, where he was featured on "Speedo Is Back". Earl, Carl, recently Billy Guy and you guessed it, Ronnie Bright,have been performing on the revival circuit,recording and knocking them dead in Las Vegas and Europe for extended engagements.

While "Speedo" was still contemplating his last exit from the group whose fame he had been most instrumental in making, the demise of The Cadillacs was gaining momentum. Milton Love from The Solitaires and Reggie Barnes, an itinerant baritone-tenor for The Fi-Tones, Solitaires,Federals, and Blue Notes were added at times. Barnes' greatest asset was that his on-stage moves were reminiscent of "Buddy"Brooks. Former Solitaires infiltrated The Cadillacs so extensively that someone decided to record the group consisting of seventy-five percent former Solitaires in the 1960's.The final Cadillacs' recording was issued in 1970 to capitalize on the revival craze.Its title perhaps suggested something about the fate of The Cadillacs.As late as mid-1972,Jimmy Bailey and Bobby Spencer with Leroy Binns and Steven Brown from The Charts were still gigging as The Cadillacs.Once J.R. Bailey

("Love, Love, Love" and "After Hours") emerged as a hot single artist and writer- publisher ("Everybody Plays The Fool"- Main Ingredient), the final curtain had rung down on the "marks of distinction" as the "mark of extinction". What had happened to one of the most exciting vocal groups ever to grace any stage? Earl Carroll has always referred to the undercurrents of "bad management" but Albert Crump, a genuine tenor whose voice exuded warmth and feeling when he was singing with The Heartbeats commented:

We had a personal manager who got twenty percent;we worked out of Gale Agency,before Shaw,and they were getting ten percent,then Shaw wanted fifteen;we had choreographers,Coles and Atkins, they got five percent. Oh, yes,you had to have new choreography for every new song.The kids wouldn't stand for the same dance steps. Then you had to have an arranger - not only for recording sessions,but for songs that were done at the clubs.There you did forty minutes to an hour, so you couldn't do just the same four or five songs that you had recorded. The arranger got five percent. You figure out what was left.[10]

What is left of The Cadillacs? Earl Carroll and J. R. Bailey have attained moderate success. The late "Buddy" Brooks was reportedly shot in 1970.The link with all those other groups, Roland Martinez, where is he today? Playing bass guitar for Cat Stevens.

Like Brooks, Carroll and company,Martinez and his brother, Joe Duncan also started out on the street corners of upper Manhattan.Martinez began with a quartet known as The Crystals. His brother was the lead of a respected uptown,frequently juke boxed Rhythm and Blues group, The Vocaleers.

The Crystals who later became The Opals, hung out on Amsterdam and St. Nicholas Avenues in the 140's at a time when young vocal groups were just beginning to emulate The Five Keys, Orioles and Ravens.One group in this neighborhood was so young that they were still listening to the "Lone Ranger" after they recorded for Robin.The Mellomoods were Ray Wooten, Bobby Baylor, Monte Owens, Bobby Williams and "Bip"Bethea. Martinez participated in this emulation of the big R&B veteran groups with John Brown of "Laugh-In"fame, Teddy Williams (the original bass)and Martin Brown.Before the group first recorded, Johnny Brown and Martinez were drafted and replaced by Johnny Hopson and Earl Wade.Hopson, Wade,Williams and Marty Brown went on to record as The Crystals for the Luna label ("Come To Me Darling"),using the

74

same background phrasing of "I Walk Alone" (Vocaleers).
When they switched to Apollo ("Oh,But She Did"/"My Heart's
Desire"), another gem,the Opal was chosen for the group's
name. Earl Wade led both sides. The "A" side, a hop-step-
jump happy tune was covered two years later in 1956 by The
El Capris (Bullseye).The Luna and Apollo ballads were sung
very slowly and were almost undanceable. Wade's voice displayed the freshness of youth but it told a sad,haunting,
dreary lament.Both of these records were top rate R&B material but in retrospect,their blues and rhythm treatments,
border on grief and dispair.

Martinez also had a short stay with The Vocaleers.In 1952-
54, The Vocaleers rivaled Jackie Robinson and Willie Mays
as Harlem folk heroes.Their turf was 142nd Street between
Amsterdam and Broadway.The original Vocaleers,before a recording contract or deal had been made with Bobby Robinson's
Red Robin label,included Herman Dunham,Joe Duncan and his
brother,Roland Martinez,someone named Ray and Beebe Cooper.
Cooper later became the bassist on "Is It A Dream", a Vocaleers' hit.As the principles of neighborhood group dynamics set in,the group reformed under the trusting guidance
of their first manager, the late Jimmy Manning. Martinez
evidently had sung with both The Opals and Vocaleers simul-
taneously, probably hopping from corner to corner.The Vocaleers who first recorded, then included Teddy Williams
(bass), Melvin Walton (Baritone), William Walker (second
tenor),Herman Dunham (the high first tenor) and Joe Duncan
(lead).In early 1952, The Vocaleers entered an Apollo amateur contest according to Herman Dunham:

> The boys and girls who heard us sing,talked the vocal
> group into trying out on amateur night.We were pretty
> lucky and took second place behind King Pleasure...
> Bobby Robinson happened to be present and heard us
> sing.He liked our sound so much that he asked us if
> we would care to record our songs.[11]

Their first record, "Be True", was a milestone in R&B
group singing.Joe Duncan could be heard warbling the blues,
almost pleading. Herman Dunham answered virtually every phrase
in falsetto voice. The piano accompaniment was similar to
The Crystals-Opals efforts of the period; the timing was
slow, the keys blue and the mood forlorn and sad. A true
hallway sound!Teddy Williams left to join The Crystals and
was replaced by Lamar Cooper on The Vocaleers' next recording, "Is It A Dream".It was during the span of this release
that The Vocaleers really began moving out as Harlem's number

one vocal group.Appearances at The Savoy Ballroom,Rockland Palace and Smalls' Paradise were not too uncommon. Unfortunately,The Vocaleers' career was to be shortlived as they recorded only two more releases after their third hit, "I Walk Alone". A gig was arranged at The Apollo but nothing came off. By 1954, another street group had begun to disintegrate.The Vocaleers had been an exceptionally good group for these early years of R&B. Their sound was primarily Rhythm and Blues;easily falling into the category of "race music".References to the "street of dreams","you left me" and "alone and blue" abounded their records.Perhaps by 1954, public tastes for a harder,driving sound had abandoned this group. But as Roland Martinez has pointed out, dissension plagued The Vocaleers just as it had undermined so many groups of the 1950's.Roland's brother, Joe, was strong headed.He had achieved stardom and understandably could not compromise. He did not want Herman Dunham to sing lead.Herman was the better virtuoso;he was more versatile and had a better voice for singing lead. However, Joe had the hit voice. Dunham just could never have made it with The Vocaleers because the public was simply used to Duncan's voice.In those days,the low budget of small independent record companies just did not facilitate the production of long playing albums where a wide range of voices could be presented.A few 78 and 45 R.P.M. releases would be made and that was usually the extent of a group's career.Herman eventually married into the family of Winston "Buzzy" Willis,a founding member of The Solitaires.The Solitaires told Herman that he could sing lead on everything. Herman took a chance with the upstart Solitaires,an amalgamation of many other groups,rejecting the chance to make more money with the more successful Vocaleers. Peer group prestige evidently,meant a lot more to Dunham than making money. Singing lead more often than just on bridges and channels,also meant something to Herman.Eventually,both The Solitaires and Vocaleers wound up making practically nothing.

Hustling on the corners of 142nd Street to get a group together was still a way of life for Martinez and Dunham. In this way,the fall from public prominence of The Vocaleers eventually paved the way for two other groups, The Vocaltones and The Solitaires.The Vocaleers did not die off completely. Hy Weiss, owner of Old Town Records had allegedly signed Dunham while he was with The Solitaires and perhaps Duncan too,as Vocaleers' records continued to appear in 1958 and 1959.[12]"I Need Your Love So Bad"(a "For Your Precious

Love" sound-a-like on Paradise), and "Love and Devotion" (Old Town) as well as "The Night Is Quiet" on Danny Robinson's Vest label were good solid up-to-date Rock 'n' Roll ballads in 1959. The Paradise item was a belated attempt to pair Dunham and Duncan as flip sided leads. By 1959, the Dunham-Duncan rift was irreparable. The heyday of The Vocaleers had passed forever.

During the beginning of The Vocaleers downfall in 1954, Roland Martinez, being forever active in the music business, decided to start dealing with another record company. He thought of Apollo Records and a group he knew from the battles in the St. Nicholas Projects on 131st Street and St. Nicholas and Seventh Avenues. The group was Miriam Grate and The Dovers. Miriam Grate Sneed, James Sneed, Eddie Quinones and Bobby Robinson (Bobby Johnson) made one record for Apollo and two for Joe Davis before fading from the public's eye. Some members of this group soon became known as The Vocaltones (a play on The Vocaleers' name) who were noted for heavy jump tunes and smooth rich ballads. They had an original sound that incorporated a shade of The Vocaleers' sad harmony. The Vocaltones were just one of the "wah-wah" Apollo groups; The Inspirations and The Keynotes were others. (Martinez played piano on the "I Don't Know" session for The Keynotes. This song was sung in the Key of G-the only key Martinez could play in 1955.)

Wyndon "Corky" Porter and Martinez formed The Vocaltones by persuading Quinones and Johnson of The Dovers to join them. They also managed to acquire the services of Miriam Grate's brother, Tommy, as a bass singer. This was the same Tommy Grate who later bassed for The Dubs, having begun on "Could This Be Magic" for Gone Records. All of The Vocaltones' four records were a gas. The jump tunes were hard, driving tough leads with smooth harmony. "I'll Never Let You Go" typified this with Martinez singing lead and Johnson the channel. The sax bridge played by Jimmy Wright, sounded as if the group was gang dancing on the corner of 142nd Street as they soul clapped and shouted. The calypso back beat prevailed on another Martinez composition, "Darling, You Know I Love You", as Martinez and Johnson reversed their lead roles. On ballads particularly "My Version Of Love", The Vocaltones' harmony emitted a throaty virile sound. Bobby Johnson's clear tenor added to this gospel-like sound. Roland remarked that The Vocaltones were four of the most beautiful cats with whom he had ever sung. They were very innocent and never, ever fooled around as some other groups were inclined.

Perhaps that is why their career was so short. After the three records for Apollo,the group suddenly broke up.Tommy Grate joined The Dubs and Eddie Quinones went on to the service. Bobby Moore and Irving Lee Gail were picked up from The Pretenders.The new Vocaltones made one more recording for George Goldner's subsidiary, Juanita(named after his daughter) in 1958."Walkin' With My Baby" displayed all The Vocaltones' traits as it skipped with a happier beat than their previous releases.It sold nothing and The Vocaltones were finished.The Goldner magic could not work for The Vocaltones as it had for the famous Flamingos, who had come to him in the same year. The Flamingos' deep R&B high tenor harmony was cleaner and more popular at End where Terry Johnson and Tommy Hunt joined Nate Nelson,Paul Wilson and the Carey cousins, Zeke and Jake. The Flamingos sound of this genre came to an end when Nate and Ray Brewster formed a group called The Starglows for Atco.

The Vocaltones were a dynamic recording group that never really got off the ground. They gigged only locally.There were no circuit tours. No big Alan Freed shows. Publicity pictures were never taken. Yet their records were played often on WWRL's "Dr. Jive" show in New York City.One way of drumming up public response to a new release was to deluge a radio station with requests and dedications.One example,the "Dr. Jive" show was the vocal group camp piece de resistance of the 1950's. Do you remember the "Vocaltone Debs",the "Channel Debs" and the "Flamingo Aces"?Everybody in a group would call the station and request their own record. Everyone's girl friends would do the same.Those fan clubs helped too. One record, "Please Say You Want Me" by The Schoolboys became a hit in this manner.Bess Berman who owned Apollo had limited resources.Keynotes',Vocaltones', Striders' records were heard on the community minded black stations but never distributed to retail outlets in white neighborhoods.Martinez related that in accounting for the Vocaltones' royalty checks,management gave them the story that they were getting something for nothing-exposure.They were told not to worry about their recording session as the company had picked up the tab.Martinez received eleven dollars for "Darling",five dollars each for "My Girl" and "I'm Gonna Get That Gal".Twenty-one dollars for an act that used to rehearse from 6:00 P.M.until 1:00 A.M.at Power Memorial High School. The Vocaltones, as well as other black vocal groups were simply not versed in the ins and outs of the music business.They knew nothing about publishing and performing rights, BMI or ASCAP. They were happy to go into a studio, hear the piano player strike up a few chords and record with "real" music in one session. But they learned! [13]

When The Vocaltones broke up, group singing was over for Roland Martinez except for a brief stint with The Solitaires. Then he started doing his own thing. After a frustrating experience with The Cadillacs at an Apollo oldies show in 1961 with The Dubs, Dell-Vikings, Miller Sisters and Solitaires, Roland threw in the towel on group singing and concentrated on other interests.

Roland and his bass guitar have been present on the recording scene ever since. Even before he tried professional singing, Roland was active with other talents. In partnership with Jimmy Jones (Pretenders), he first influenced and paid for The Elchords' session at Gofarb's Studios for Good Records; a session that was to produce a very controversial recording. Butchie Saunders (lead), Bernard Johnson (first tenor), Elliot Johnson (second tenor), Raphael (?) (baritone) and Cookie (?) (bass), put together "Peppermint Stick", a Frankie Lymon type song that was banned because of its overly suggestive lyric. Roland remembered the Cholly Atkins' choreography and taught it to The Royaltones ("Crazy Love"-Old Town) from Brooklyn and to The Ebonaires ("Love Call"-Lena) from the 144-150 and Amsterdam area of Manhattan. His earliest achievement was believing in a relatively unknown Apollo group, The Chesters. He rehearsed them at his house and then took them to Richard Barrett at End Records. The group became known as Little Anthony and The Imperials. Roland has since taken his street experiences and put them to work for Lloyd Price. [14]

Another New York group whose history, music, origin and personnel were closely tied to The Cadillacs and Vocaleers, were the "Walkin' Along" men, The Solitaires. All of the original Solitaires had come from other groups; The Crows, Mellomoods, Four Bells, Concords and Vocaleers. Yet The Solitaires had a distinctive sound. They were not a dancing group. They didn't wow the audience with fancy footwork. Like The Five Keys, they just stood around a microphone and sang their hearts out. Most record companies considered a quintet as nothing more than a lead voice with a background. The Solitaires defied this shortsighted outlook. Even though they had as many as four different lead singers;their sound was always identifiable.It was always easy to recognize a Solitaires' new release.This was a group that felt its music.

In 1954, when Herman Dunham left The Vocaleers,he went looking for a greener pasture on 142nd Street.Street corner singing, a way of life in 1954 on this street, became emblazoned with excitement when a local group made black music history.Bill Davis,Daniel "Sonny" Norton,Harold Major and Gerald Hamilton had formed a bird group called The Crows. Davis had written a song called "Gee" that was recorded by George Goldner (Rama).[15]The song became the first recording of black street corner singing to transcend the realm of R&B into the white pop market.It was a million seller and the first "doo-wop" record to be recognized by the white media. In hindsight, it has often been referred to as the first group Rock 'n' Roll record. Goldner paid tribute to this landmark by naming another label, Gee, after the song.The Crows who were famous in Harlem for their big '55 Chrysler with "Crows" painted on the side tried to invade the white entertainment world through other avenues.Their attempt for example,to perform before white audiences in Las Vegas met with failure.Las Vegas was not ready for this early bridging of cultural gaps.According to Martinez,it was not until The Spaniels (VeeJay) performed in Las Vegas,that the relationship between black music and white audiences was accepted.The Crows made other records;"Untrue","Heartbreaker", "I Really Really Love You" and the commercial spoof of a local wine commercial,"Mambo Shevitz".As The Crows passed rapidly into relative obscurity, their recordings have emerged as sure fire collectors' items.Today,both Hamilton,the bass, and Norton,the lead are deceased.Only proud memories remain for Davis and Major.

A young Winston Willis, rumors persist,used to sing on the stoops of 142nd Street, with his idols and pals, The Crows.Willis never recorded with The Crows but it is safe to assume that Willis frequently jammed with them. As The Crows began to die out,they were replaced by The Solitaires as the kings of the Street.This block,142nd Street between 7th Avenue and Lenox Avenue,was loaded with group singers. Buzzy, who became the spokesman for The Solitaires,met up with former members from several groups. Pat Gaston from The Four Bells (Gem), Bobby Baylor, Bobby Williams and Monte Owens from The Mellomoods (Red Robin),all tested out their vocal chords on 142nd Street and at P.S.139. When

Herman Dunham came around,this nomadic gallery was complete. Their style was always unique, except for one song which was led by Bobby Williams, who died in 1961. "Shoobie" as his friends called him,led only one number,"I Don't Stand A Ghost Of A Chance" which bore familiarity to an unreleased version by The Five Keys.The Keys and Solitaires probably rehearsed this song while on the road together."Shoobie's" voice was full ranged and silky. It warbled with a ghost-like wavering.

The original Solitaires,a real "Solid New York Group", first included Herman Dunham (lead),Bobby Williams (piano and first tenor),Bobby Baylor(second tenor),Winston "Buzzy" Willis (baritone),Pat Gaston (bass)and Monte Owens (guitar). "Solid New York Group" was a special term reserved only for those groups whose melodies provoked feelings of closeness to city life and a longing for a lost loved one. The Sol-itaires' voices,particularly on "The Angels Sang" sounded as if they were chapel bells echoing from rooftops.It was not difficult to visualize tenements, brownstones, busy streets shrouded in the shadows of the New York skyline. Herman Dunham had found his niche with The Solitaires. He led on eight of the first ten Solitaires' sides,singing on each of them like a thrush.He was smooth,almost child-like on"Wonder Why";rich,powerful and lusty on those slow grinds, "Please Remember My Heart" and "My Dear".When he returned from the Air Force in 1956,he was mellow again on "Please Kiss This Letter", the song The Harptones never recorded. In 1958,on "Honey Babe",he was belting and booming again. No one ever sang harder than Herman Dunham.On the simplest lyric, he exuded feeling and power.Could he sing!

In addition to Dunham,there were other lead voices"Shoobie" on "Ghost" and Bobby Baylor on the latin-blues version of "South Of The Border". In 1955, when Dunham was drafted, Milton Love was added. Love was a Solitaire in style, but his voice added a new dimension on record. His tenor was sweeter than Dunham's.He and Baylor immediately began their satirical duets on "The Wedding" and "The Honeymoon".At in person appearances,Milton wore a mop over his head to play the female role in the routine.In 1955,Monte Owens' guitar was added to the shuffling "Later For You Baby". In 1956,the honeymoon was over for Pat Gaston as he was drafted and re-placed by the deep-voiced former Cricket, Fred Barksdale. Barksdale came to be a Solitaire through circumstances more ludicrous than the group's routine on "The Wedding".

Within a month after the final break-up of The Crickets

in 1956, Barksdale went to see a show at The Apollo where he always worshipped at the shrine of his favorite R&B stars; Sonny Til,Clyde McPhatter and Jimmy Ricks. In the two years that Barksdale had spent with The Crickets, he had never performed on The Apollo stage.Barksdale did not know it on this day in 1956 but his dream of appearing at The Apollo was soon to be realized.Upon leaving the theatre, he went down to the basement to use the men's room where he met an old friend,"Buzzy" Willis.Having remembered Fred from bas- ketball and The Velvetones at the St.Phillip's and St.Mark's Churches, Willis invited him to a rehearsal. Fred went to the Polo Grounds (Colonial) projects on 158th Street and 8th Avenue to start singing with Love,Willis,Owens and Baylor. The realization of his dream was just around the corner.16

"Nothing Like A Little Love" revealed Fred's first effort with The Solitaires.Next came that foot stompin' New York sounding million seller for The Solitaires,"Walkin' Along". It took The Solitaires right to The Apollo and right to the mailbox to receive their first and only royalty check;ap- proximately two hundred dollars per man. Barksdale remem- bered: "To this day we never thought it ("Walkin' Along") would do very much. We did it just to be doing a record. We needed something to back up "No More Sorrows" ("Please Kiss This Letter"). We had no routine for it."17

After the fame and some fortune of "Walkin' Along",which was covered by the kings of group cover records,The Diamonds (Mercury), The Solitaires went back to ballads and the same old story.There was no money.Prohibitive costs of recording sessions supposedly yielded no royalties. After the shock of the "Walkin' Along" royalty check, The Solitaires just kept singing for the love of it.18 They recorded R&B standards, "The Bells" (Dominoes), "At Night" (Orioles) and a newie, "Hully Gully Roll" that were never released.This group was so versatile that they should have been like The Temptations today.19 "No More Sorrows", "Embraceable You" and "Thrill Of Love" achieved very limited success.An album was supposed to have been released by Old Town but it fell to the wayside with the surge of pop-jazz singer, Arthur Prysock on the label. Fred reported that individual members of the group had signed separate contracts at different times with Old Town, thus preventing them from breaking contract collec- tively.This was supposedly done to get personal advances. The Solitaires then refused to make any more records. "Buzzy" started appearing with The Moonglows. The last Solitaires groups to perform included a girl,Cathy Miller,and today's revival members: Bobby,Milton and Fred."Buzzy" began producing for various recording companies: MGM, Roulette and RCA.Today, he is in charge of Rhythm and Blues production at RCA,thanks to the guidance of Hy Weiss who believed in him.In 1964,"Buzzy" gave his old pals a chance at Roulette. "Buzzy" produced and Cecil Holmes(Fi-Tones) conducted the orchestra for The Chances ("Through A Long And Sleepless Night"). Milton sang lead as he was accompanied by Bobby Baylor, Reggie Barnes, Roland Martinez, Fred Barksdale,[20] Cecil Holmes and a stranger in the studio who added the "didda-dit"bass,ruining an excellent comeback recording.

After The Solitaires had "Big Mary's House" released in 1958, they took their green suits,white shoes and red ties to the New York Paramount for a show with Ted Steele.They had stopped wearing their plaid jackets rented·from the same agency where The Moonglows and Four Fellows had rented the same uniform. They were to appear on this show with Clyde McPhatter, The "Big Bopper", Buddy Holly and The Crickets and Frankie Avalon.Then the infamous plane crash occurred. Ed "For Your Love" Townsend and Jerry Butler and The Impressions were brought in as replacements for "The Bopper" and Holly.The audience wouldn't let The Solitaires off the stage but the real show stopper was a new group,The Impressions, who were called back three times to do "For Your Precious Love" and "Sweet Was The Wine".People asked:"Who's the cat singing high tenor-is that a girl?"[21]The answer was Curtis Mayfield.

In 1958,a new Rhythm and Blues tradition was being created while an old one was fading away.

SOLITAIRES DISCOGRAPHY AND PERSONNEL

OLD TOWN

1000	WONDER WHY/BLUE VALENTINE	Herman Dunham
1006	PLEASE REMEMBER MY HEART/	Bobby Williams
	SOUTH OF THE BORDER	Bobby Baylor
1008	CHANCES I'VE TAKEN/LONELY	Buzzy Willis
1010	I DON'T STAND A GHOST OF A	Monte Owens
	CHANCE/GIRL OF MINE	Pat Gaston
1012	WHAT DID SHE SAY/MY DEAR	

1014	THE WEDDING/DON'T FALL IN LOVE	Milton Love
1015	MAGIC ROSE/LATER FOR YOU BABY	Monte Owens
1019	THE HONEYMOON/FINE LITTLE GIRL	Bobby Baylor
		Buzzy Willis
		Pat Gaston
		Bobby Williams

1026	YOU'VE SINNED/THE ANGELS SANG	Milton Love
	(YOU'RE BACK WITH ME)	Monte Owens
1032	GIVE ME ONE MORE CHANCE	Bobby Baylor
		Buzzy Willis
		Pat Gaston

1032	NOTHING LIKE A LITTLE LOVE	Milton Love
1034	WALKIN' ALONG	Monte Owens
		Bobby Baylor
		Buzzy Willis
		Fred Barksdale

1034	PLEASE KISS THIS LETTER	Herman Dunham
		Milton Love
		Bobby Baylor
		Buzzy Willis
		Fred Barksdale
		Monte Owens

1044	I REALLY LOVE YOU SO	Milton Love
	(HONEY BABE)/THRILL OF LOVE	Herman Dunham
		Bobby Baylor
		Buzzy Willis
		Monte Owens

1049	WALKIN' AND TALKIN'	Milton Love
		Herman Dunham
		Bobby Baylor
		Buzzy Willis
		Wally Roker

1049 NO MORE SORROWS   Milton Love
                                        Herman Dunham
                                        Bobby Baylor
                                        Buzzy Willis
                                        Fred Barksdale

1059 BIG MARY'S HOUSE   Milton Love
                                        Monte Owens
                                        Bobby Baylor
                                        Buzzy Willis
                                        Pat Gaston
                                        Bobby Williams

1059 PLEASE REMEMBER MY HEART   Milton Love
1066 EMBRACEABLE YOU/   Bobby Baylor
        'ROUND GOES MY HEART   Buzzy Willis
                                        Monte Owens
                                        Fred Barksdale

1071 HELPLESS/LIGHT A CANDLE IN   Milton Love
        THE CHAPEL   Fred Barksdale
1096 LONESOME LOVER/PRETTY THING   Monte Owens
1139 TIME IS HERE   Reggie Barnes
                                        Cecil Holmes
                                        Roland Martinez

1139 HONEY BABE   See OLD TOWN 1044

ARGO

5316 WALKIN' ALONG/   See OLD TOWN 1034
        PLEASE KISS THIS LETTER
                            both previous listings

<u>ROULETTE</u>   THE CHANCES

4549	THROUGH A LONG AND SLEEPLESS NIGHT/WHAT WOULD YOU SAY	Milton Love Bobby Baylor Reggie Barnes Roland Martinez Fred Barksdale Cecil Holmes

<u>MGM</u>   THE SOLITAIRES

K13221	FOOL THAT I AM/ FAIR WEATHER LOVER	Milton Love Cecil Holmes Reggie Barnes Buzzy Willis Bobby Baylor

CADILLACS' DISCOGRAPHY AND PERSONNEL[22]

JOSIE

765	I WONDER WHY/GLORIA	Earl Carroll
769	WISHING WELL/I WANT TO KNOW ABOUT LOVE	Laverne Drake
		James Clark
		"Gus" Willingham
		Bobby Phillips
773	NO CHANCE/SYMPATHY	Earl Carroll
778	DOWN THE ROAD/WINDOW LADY	Laverne Drake
785	LET ME EXPLAIN/SPEEDOO	Earl Wade
792	ZOOM/YOU ARE	Charles Brooks
		Bobby Phillips
798	BETTY MY LOVE/WOE IS ME	Earl Carroll
805	(THAT'S ALL) I NEED/THE GIRL I LOVE	James Bailey
807	SHOCK-A-DOO/RUDOLPH THE RED NOSED REINDEER [23]	Earl Wade
		Charles Brooks
812	ABOUT THAT GIRL NAMED LOU/ SUGAR-SUGAR	Bobby Phillips
820	BROKEN HEART/MY GIRL FRIEND	James Bailey
		Robert Spencer
		Bill Lindsay
		Champ Rollow

THE ORIGINAL CADILLACS

821	HURRY HOME/LUCY	Earl Carroll
		Earl Wade
		Charles Brooks
		Bobby Phillips

EARL CARROLL AND THE ORIGINAL CADILLACS

829	BUZZ-BUZZ-BUZZ/YEA YEA BABY	Earl Carroll
		James Bailey
		Earl Wade
		Charles Brooks
		Bobby Phillips

JESSE POWELL AND THE CADDY'S

834	TURNPIKE(Instr.)/ AIN'T YOU GONNA	James Bailey
		Robert Spencer

                                                    Bill Lindsay
                                                    Champ Rollow

836 SPEEDO IS BACK/A' LOOKA HERE   Earl Carroll
842 HOLY SMOKE BABY/I WANT TO KNOW   James Bailey
846 PEEK-A-BOO/OH, OH LOLITA   Robert Spencer
857 JAY WALKER/COPY CAT   Earl Wade
861 PLEASE,MR. JOHNSON/COOL IT FOOL   Bobby Phillips

                SPEEDO AND THE PEARLS
865 WHO YA GONNA KISS/NAGGITY NAG   Earl Carroll
                                                    Howard Guyton
                                                    Derek Martin
                                                    George Torrence
                                                    Coley Washington

866 ROMEO/ALWAYS MY DARLING   Robert Spencer
870 BIG DAN McGOON/DUMBELL   Earl Wade
                                                    James Bailey
                                                    Bobby Phillips

              SPEEDO AND THE CADILLACS
876 TELL ME TODAY/IT'S LOVE   Earl Carroll
                                                    Roland Martinez
                                                    Kirk Davis
                                                    Ronnie Bright

883 THAT'S WHY/THE BOOGIE MAN   Reggie Barnes
                                                    Roland Martinez
                                                    Earl Carroll
                                                    Bobby Phillips

               THE ORIGINAL CADILLACS
915 I'LL NEVER LET YOU GO/   Earl Wade
        WAYWARD WANDERER   Roland Martinez
                                                    Junior Glanton
                                                    Bobby Phillips

SMASH
1712 WHAT YOU BET/YOU ARE TO BLAME   Earl Carroll
                                                    Ray Brewster
                                                    Roland Martinez
                                                    Curtis Williams
                                                    Irving Lee Gail

                         88

CAPITOL
4825　WHITE GARDENIA/GROOVY GROOVY LOVE

Roland Martinez
Robert Spencer
James Bailey
Ray Brewster

BOBBY RAY AND THE CADILLACS
4835　LA BOMBA/I SAW YOU

Ray Brewster
Roland Martinez
Robert Spencer
James Bailey

ARTIC
101　FOOL/THE RIGHT KIND OF LOVIN'

Milton Love
Ray Brewster
Bobby Baylor
Fred Barksdale

MERCURY
71738 I'M WILLING/THRILL ME SO

Earl Carroll
Robert Spencer
Roland Martinez
Reggie Barnes
Milton Love

POLYDOR　·　THE ORIGINAL CADILLACS
14031 DEEP IN THE HEART OF THE GHETTO
　　　Parts 1 & 2

Bobby Phillips
Robert Spencer
James Bailey
Leroy Binns
Eddie Jones (piano)

MIRIAM GRATE AND THE DOVERS' DISCOGRAPHY

APOLLO

472	MY ANGEL/PLEASE SQUEEZE	Miriam Grate
		James Sneed
		Eddie Quinones
		Bobby Johnson

DAVIS

465	BOY IN MY LIFE/SWEET AS A FLOWER	Miriam Grate
NEW HORIZON		James Sneed
501	THE SENTENCE/DEVIL YOU MAY BE	Eddie Quinones
		Wyndon Porter

VOCALTONES' DISCOGRAPHY AND PERSONNEL

APOLLO

488	I'M GONNA GET THAT GAL/	Bobby Robinson
	MY GIRL	Roland Martinez
492	THREE KINDS OF PEOPLE/	Wyndon Porter
	DARLING (YOU KNOW I LOVE YOU)	Eddie Quinones
497	I'LL NEVER LET YOU GO/	Tommy Grate
	MY VERSION OF LOVE	

JUANITA

100	WALKIN' WITH MY BABY/	Bobby Robinson
	WANNA LEE	Roland Martinez
		Wyndon Porter
		Bobby Moore
		Irving Lee Gail

RED ROBIN

113	BE TRUE/OH! WHERE	Joe Duncan
		Herman Dunham
		William Walker
		Melvin Walton
		Teddy Williams

114	IS IT A DREAM/HURRY HOME	Joe Duncan
119	I WALK ALONE/HOW SOON	Herman Dunham
		William Walker
		Melvin Walton
		Lamar Cooper

125	WILL YOU BE TRUE/LOVE YOU	Joe Duncan
		Herman Dunham
		Melvin Walton
		Lamar Cooper

132	ANGEL FACE/LOVIN' BABY	Joe Duncan
		Joe Powell
		Melvin Walton
		Lamar Cooper

PARADISE

113	I NEED YOUR LOVE SO BAD/	Joe Duncan
	HAVE YOU EVER LOVED SOMEONE	Herman Dunham
		Melvin Walton
		Richard Blandon
		Lamar Cooper

OLD TOWN

1089	LOVE AND DEVOTION/	Joe Duncan
	THIS IS THE NIGHT	Herman Dunham
		Melvin Walton
		Leo"Tiny" Fuller

VEST

832	THE NIGHT IS QUIET/HEAR MY PLEA	Melvin Walton
		Joe Duncan
		William Walker
		Leo Fuller
		Caesar Williams

TWISTIME
11   COOTIE SNAP/ A GOLDEN TEAR   Melvin Walton
                                                William Walker
                                                Curtis Blandon
                                                Leo Fuller

ROSE
17   ONE ROOM/ I WONDER   THE STYLISTS
                                                Joe Duncan
                                                Rudy Cooper
                                                Sonny Garrett
                                                Alvin Black
                                                Lamar Cooper

[1] Interview with Earl Carroll, May 10, 1971.

[2] The street Carnations, according to J.R. Bailey, consisted of Earl Carroll, Bobby Phillips, Laverne Drake and "Cub", as bass. William Dempsey identified the original Cadillacs' picture as Earl, Bobby, Laverne, "Poppa" Clark, and "Gus" Willingham. Willingham's brother, J.B., sang with The Pastels and his sister sang the "big ol' lump o' sugar" role with The Hearts.

[3] Interviews with J.R. Bailey, September 10, 1971 and Fred Barksdale, October 1, 1971.

[4] Interview with Bobby Thomas, August 28, 1971.

[5] Bim Bam Boom, Vol. I, Number 5.

[6] It has been reputed that The Mills Brothers were the first to record "Gloria".

[7] Interviews with Roland Martinez, October 10, 1971 and April 29, 1971.

[8] Fred Barksdale interviewed by Tom Luciani, WFUV-FM, November 26, 1970 and interview with Fred Barksdale, Oct. 1, 1971.

[9] Cholly Atkins remarked that The Cadillacs' dance routines were not different than others except that "we adhered to the rhythmic patterns of their tunes. Their songs had great rhythm tracks. The Cadillacs were very flexible and responded beautifully to dictation which made them unique. They had great precision. At that time there were very few acts that moved precisely. A lot of them moved but not with precision." Interview with Charles Atkinson, March 5, 1973.

[10] Jeff Beckman, "The Heartbeats...Continued", Big Town Review, Vol. I, Number 3, July-August, 1972, Page 18.

[11] Herman Dunham interviewed by Tom Denehy (unpublished), 1971.

[12] Barksdale, October 1, 1971.

[13]Martinez,April 29,1971.

[14]Ibid.

[15]Jeff Beckman and Hank Feigenbaum,"Gee,It's The Crows", Big Town Review,Vol.I,Number 2,April-May,1972,Page 31.

[16]Barksdale,November 26,1970.

[17]Ibid.

[18]Ibid.

[19]Interview with Hy Weiss,July 27,1971.

[20]Barksdale's last recording effort was with Champ Rollow, Ronnie Bright, Bob Spencer, and Jimmy Bailey, all our old friends, as The Crystals who backed up Sam Hawkins on "King Of Fools" (Gone 5042).

[21]Barksdale.

[22]A large portion of personnel information in discographies comes from Roland Martinez and Milton Love.

[23]"That's All I Need" and "Sugar-Sugar" have early master numbers, 075 and 078, indicating that Drake and not Bailey sang on these cuts.

Chapter 6

The Kingdom of Rhythm and Blues

"Tin Pan Alley",Memphis,Hollywood,Detroit and the South side of Chicago,have all been recognized as fertile crescents of American popular music. In the 1950's, there was one neighborhood that probably contributed more to popular music generally and Rhythm and Blues specifically,than many have ever recognized.In Manhattan,115th Street from Fifth Avenue to as far west as Eighth Avenue, was the spawning ground for several Rhythm and Blues vocal groups.It would have been possible to walk down 115th Street in 1955 and pass groups singing on the corners of Fifth, Lenox,Seventh,St. Nicholas and Eighth Avenues.The phenomenon of street corner singing whether it had been on the open stage of the street, or in the shadows of the Wadley and Cooper Junior High Schools was indeed a way of life in the mid-fifties;a way of life that prolifically produced the greatest number of recording groups ever to come from one neighborhood.Unlike the Fremont High groups of Los Angeles (Penguins,Dootones,Medallions, Hollywood Flames) that all seemed to have a similarly identifiable sound,the 115th Street groups developed styles that were all different from one another. There were "doo-wop" groups, pop-jazz groups, soft ballad groups, rough voiced jump tune groups and adolescent high tenor groups. It was definitely probable that on any given night the city air and street noises would be serenaded by the sounds of The Five Crowns, The Harptones,The Wanderers,The Willows,The Channels,The Bop-chords, The Ladders, The Laddins,The Charts, The Whirlers, The Cellos, The Matadors, and The Keynotes. Not too far away in the man-made echo chamber under the elevated railroad tracks of The New York Central on Park Avenue and 119th Street were The Schoolboys, The Jesters and The Desires.

Why was this neighborhood so rich in a culture that blossomed before being subjected to commercial exploitation,personal disappointment and eventual extinction from the street corners of New York City?There had been the "pied pipers"; both human and man made.The records blaring out from record stores on 116th, 125th, 135th and 149th Streets;the talent shows at churches and schools;and the stars;Sonny Til,Jimmy Ricks,Clyde McPhatter,and Nate Nelson;all made impressions on the young folk of the neighborhoods. Such hit records as "Sunday Kind Of Love"/"I'll Never Tell"(Harptones),"Church Bells May Ring" (Willows),and "Wrong Party Again." (Singing Wanderers) added promise to the hopes and aspirations of those young street corner singers who were to follow.

The Five Crowns were supposedly the first,The Harptones were the best and later The Drifters (Crowns) were the most successful to emerge from this street. One of the first groups in the neighborhood was not a Rhythm and Blues group but was classified in the pop-jazz vein.

In 1972,The Joe Cuba Sextet recorded a song called "Do You Feel It". The record was about El Barrio (East Harlem or Spanish Harlem),a neighborhood that stretches from approximately 96th to 125th Streets,and from First to Fifth Avenues. The lead singer who could feel the pulse of this neighborhood in his bones was Ray Pollard,the same man who had been the lead singer of The Singing Wanderers. This early pop-jazz group came from 116th Street and Lenox Avenue,just one block west of the neighborhood its lead singer was describing in 1972.

Alfonso Brown(lead), Frank Joyner(second tenor),Robert Yarborough(baritone) and Sheppard Grant(bass),began as The Barons and then later became The Larks while pursuing their amateur singing careers in an old record shop on 116th Street. It was not until the group won an amateur contest at The Apollo that their name was changed to The Singing Wanderers. In 1952,The Singing Wanderers,patterning themselves after the "good music" of The Mills Brothers,had progressed no further than the proverbial hallway echo chamber. They asked returning Korean War veteran,Ray Pollard,who had gone to Cooper Junior High School with Frank Joyner,if he would like to help out with the harmony as Alfonso Brown was not making rehearsals. The result was "Could We Find Happiness"/ "Hey Meh Ethel" (Savoy 1109) and "Wrong Party Again"/"Say Hey Willie Mays" (Decca). Through the wise management of Lee Magid(Savoy Records), they worked in a pop-jazz bag, touring with Ethel Merman, Martha Raye and Eartha Kitt. The Singing Wanderers appeared on the Ed Sullivan Show five times in 1954-55. They were allegedly the first black group to do choreography on the Sullivan Show. It was during one tour that The Singing Wanderers suffered an experience that was not too uncommon to the hardships one might expect with one night stands. While en route to Las Vegas from Chicago one winter, they found themselves trapped in an incredible snow storm. Twenty foot drifts obscured their vision of everything but the tops of telephone poles. They were stuck for four to five days with nothing but potato chips and "life savers".Pollard was lucky enough to find an old farmhouse where they kept warm one day until the owner came and tractored them four miles to the nearest town, Middle City, Kansas. The hotels were filled with stranded travelers.The four Wanderers were given lodging-in the city jail!

The group laid low for some years until Sammy Lowe at Onyx Records convinced them to record again. The name was shortened to The Wanderers as Ray Pollard's powerful,rich voice led through "Thinking Of You".This record permanently established Ray's reputation as one of the most versatile lead singers of all time.He possessed a full range of vocal octaves from bass to tenor. This style was repeated again on The Wanderers' greatest hit, the remake of the old Ed Townsend standard "For Your Love" in 1960 for Cub (MGM).The Wanderers recorded eighteen sides for Cub (MGM) until the group finally broke up with the passing away of Shep Grant in May of 1970.Ray continued his singing career and in 1971, appeared in the Broadway production of "Purlie".[1]Ray Pollard is one of the few fifties lead singers whose voice has maintained its pitch and gusto through the years. To hear him sing today is a shattering and thrilling experience.

While appearing at The Apollo in 1956, on the strength of "Thinking Of You", The Wanderers were managed by Tommy Smalls.This was the only time that The Wanderers were classified as a Rhythm and Blues group.Because of their permanent pop-jazz groove, the group lost some of its appeal to the teenage record buying public of the mid-fifties.They probably also lost peer following in the neighborhood around 116th Street.

One group that did have a profound effect on the neighborhood youngsters was The Five Willows.

Two blocks away on 114th Street lived a young man who was later to appear in "Purlie" with Ray Pollard and Milton Grayson (Dominoes). One day in 1952, while Tony Middleton was polishing up his boxing skills at a local gymnasium,he was invited to Mrs. Clarisse Martin's house on 115th Street where her twin sons,Joe and Ralph;Richie Davis;John Thomas "Scooter" Steele;and a young Bobby Robinson (of Red Robin-Whirlin Disc-Fury fame) were rehearsing. Mrs. Martin knew that if she could teach the boys diligence and discipline, they could someday achieve at least some element of status in the entertainment world.She would make the group practice every day to pass the time and keep the youngsters off the street. When not under her immediate attention,they would sing in the hallway of their building, or in hospitals,at church benefits and at some dances at The Chelsea Vocational High School. There were rehearsals with some girls called The Delltones.One member of The Delltones was Gloria Lynne who went on to become the very famous jazz singer.

On some occasions,a member of The Five Crowns,Dock Green would walk over from 7th Avenue to join with the group known at this time as The Dovers. Green used to sing often with The Dovers especially his favorite,"The Wiffenpoof Song", which had been recorded by The Cabineers (Abbey).The original Five Willows;Tony Middleton(lead),Richie Davis(first tenor), Ralph Martin (second tenor),Joe Martin (baritone)and"Scooter"(bass),went to Pete and Goldie Durain to record four mild early R&B hits including the street song,"My Dear, Dearest Darling" for Allen Records (formerly Abbey). The Willows' records were famous for their bass intro's and breaks.The "bah-bah" beginning by "Scooter" on "My Dear Dearest Darling" was to be continued later on "Little Darlin'" and "Do You Love Me".[2]

The recording that made The Willows,the one that established their heavy,"willowy" sound was the famous fifties rocker, "Church Bells May Ring".This record had all the ingredients of a fifties' smash; the five part harmony, the surging beat, the talking bass break,the fade away ending and Tony's rough and ready lead.Ironically,the most famous Willows' bass bridge, "Hello, hello again, my friend I'm hopin' that we'll meet again", was sung by Richard Simon, a neighborhood pal who just did that one session. "Church Bells" was a million seller for The Willows who received writers' credit for the song. It was extensively covered by Sunny Gale, The Cadets and of course, The Diamonds. It has been said that The Willows had to sue for their writers' royalties.They were awarded $200.00-divided five ways for a million seller![3]

The Willows went on to record a few more sides before Tony Middleton began an extensive recording and stage career.[4]The rest of The Willows with Richie Davis doing lead, stayed around until 1964 when they recorded two medium sized R&B hits for Heidi (an Atco subsidiary),"It's Such A Shame" and "Sit By The Fire".For a while it seemed like old times with Freddie Donovan bassing his way through the fade out on "Sit By The Fire".

The Willows may have made some impression on teenaged music lovers by Middleton's boss lead, or by the fast uptempo beat of their songs or by the first use of chimes on a Rock'n'Roll record (played incidentally by a very young singer-writer named Neil Sedaka). The real impact of The Willows on the youth of the neighborhood may have been in the fact that The Willows lived in Mrs. Martin's house on 115th Street with others who later turned out to be members of The Bop-chords, Channels and Ladders. By 1955, The Five Crowns, Harptones and possibly The Wanderers had had their successes. The real R&B idols on 115th Street were The Willows. The Martin brothers, Freddie Donovan and Richie Davis lived in the same building with Morris "Mickey" Smarr. "Mickey" and his pals, Ernest Harriston(lead), William Dailey(first tenor), Ken "Butch" Hamilton (second tenor) and Leon Ivey (bass) were the teenage rage of 115th Street for being so good looking, hangin' out and singin' street songs on the corners of Lenox Avenue. But when "Church Bells May Ring" came out, the girls started drifting to The Willows. Envy prompted "Mickey", Ernie and the rest of The Bop-Chords to make records. Freddie Donovan brought The Bop-Chords to Danny Robinson, Bobby Robinson's brother, who was starting a new label called Holiday.[5]Robinson liked The Bop-Chords and recorded one of their street songs, "Castle In The Sky". It was one of those instant mild New York group smashes:it had the melodic New York lead and everything worked-the record hops, the church dances and the radio dedications and requests. "Castle In The Sky" sold approximately 150,000 records. Not bad for a small independent record company and a group of kids from the neighborhood block in 1956. On the strength of "Castle", The Bop-Chords went into The Apollo on July 26, 1956, for a week's engagement. In those days, groups worked long hours (7,8 or 9 shows a day,7 days a week) for modest wages (approximately $900.00 for the week, divided five ways). But who cared? The whole fun of it was making records, being loved by the people and performing on that world famous stage. The Bop-Chords' second record, "When I Woke Up This Morning", was even better;but sold only 75-100,000 copies. Finally,in 1957,this group grew disgusted too,disbanding and picking up replacements,Peggy Jones and "Skip" Boyd.Ernest,"Butch",Peggy and "Skip" made one more record as The Bop-Chords, "So Why" in 1957.Ernest continued to record as a back-up singer and occasional fill-in for Shep and The Limelites and The Lovenotes. He recorded "We Need Love" and "Tell It To Me" as Ernie Johnson for Asnes in 1962.[6]

Living upstairs over The Bop-Chords on 115th Street,was a group whose nucleus was built around first tenor, Herb

Jennings, two brothers, Douglas Jackson(bass), and Johnny Jackson(lead), Irvin Jones(high tenor),and Ron Clark(baritone). In 1958, they also recorded for Danny Robinson in a strange style that seemed to have a bass dominated harmony that repeated "ya,ya" over and over.The Ladders' soaring first tenor on "I Want To Know" (Holiday- Everlast Publishing) and their only other release "My Love Is Gone" (Vest - Everlast Publishing), an updated version of the theme from "Gone With The Wind", was some of the best high octave tenoring ever recorded on group records. The significance about The Ladders, is that their manager, Les Cooper,arranged "I Want To Know" in the same vocal patterns as he had arranged "Deserie" (Everlast) for The Charts,another 115th Street group. Cooper himself had been a member of a group that recorded as The Empires for Harlem, Wing, Whirlin Disc ("Linda"),Amp 3 ("If I'm A Fool") and as The Whirlers for Whirlin Disc. On "Magic Mirror", John Barnes sang lead for The Whirlers with Cooper as first tenor,Robert Dunn as second tenor and baritone, and William Toddman as bass.In 1960,Cooper made his mark with a smash instrumental called "Wiggle Wobble" on Everlast.The tenor hornman on that record was the former lead singer of The Charts.[7]

When Les Cooper met The Charts,they were not exactly the most polished group around.They had just finished an abominable showing at The Apollo amateur night for which they were booed off the stage for singing a weird song."Deserie" was a drag as it "wah-wahed" along with no channel.The Charts (originally eight or nine fellows off the street), Joseph Grier(lead), Steven Brown(first tenor), Glenmore Jackson, (second tenor),Leroy Binns(baritone),and Ross Buford(bass) were just five guys who literally grew tired of gang fighting and had turned to singing as a hobby.They knew nothing about a channel having to be in a song.The channel or bridge of an R&B song,particularly a ballad,occurred usually in the middle or last third of the lyrics.It featured a change in tempo, a slight change in melody,more romantic words than the rest of the song and it climaxed with a resounding return to the regular harmony pattern of the song.Apollo patrons or any audience could really judge how well a group could go into a channel and then return to the main melody of a song.Nothing was more exciting than to see five guys putting their hearts together in a song while the audience was shouting their approval. Grier, Cooper, or Robinson, either intentionally or inadvertently, omitted a channel from "Deserie".The Charts just came out on the stage,sang that continuous "wah-wah" melody right through the boo's, on to the Everlast label and into three and a half million copies sold of the novel recording. No hanging around corners any more and no one-nighters in downtown nightclubs for these guys. They were an immediate smash. But The Charts were too young. The youngest, Brown, was 13, and the oldest, Grier was 19. Grier, too unfamiliar with the workings of the music business, sold the writer's rights to the song. The Charts lost out on most of the royalties. After four more records for Everlast, including "You're The Reason", and "Dance Girl", The Charts faded away. In April, 1966, a revamped Charts with Binns, Brown, Tony Harris, and Frankie Fears, tried to do an up-tempo version, "Desiree" on Wand. The total demise of The Charts, a group that had some alumni of Charles Evans Hughes High School (West 18th Street in Manhattan), had been completed. Many R&B acts that had attended Hughes were only memories of the past by 1966. At one time or another, some or all of the members of The Cellos, Johnnie and Joe, The Kodoks, Schoolboys, Metronomes, Keynotes, and The Hearts (with "Baby" Washington), had passed through the halls of the school.[8]

Although The Charts had risen to popularity inadvertently by not singing an R&B channel, there was one unique New York group that based its style and name solely around the musical term. The Channels featured the three part harmony of the group out front ahead of the bass and top tenor. The tenor took the lead only in the channel on "The Closer You Are" and "The Gleam In Your Eye". The Channels had created a brand new approach to New York street songs in a perfected style that has never been duplicated.

In 1955, Earl Lewis (tenor) and Clifton Wright (bass), members of a group called The Lotharios, were at a talent show at a community center on 101st Street at Columbus and Amsterdam Avenues. The audience was dominated by Frankie Lymon fans who had come to see The Teenagers and not some upstart group. The Lotharios were forced to leave the stage in favor of The Teenagers. Three members of The Channels from 115th and 116th Streets, approached Lewis and Wright to join their group as lead and bass. The next neighborhood talent show at P.S. 113 on 113th Street, saw The Channels (Earl Lewis, Edward Dolphin, Billy Morris, Larry Hamptden and Clifton Wright) win singing the old Flamingos' standard, "I'll Be Home". On the following Wednesday, they took second place, singing "The Magic Touch" at The Apollo, and being noticed by Bobby Robinson. They auditioned for his Whirlin

Disc label with one of the finer but lesser known groups from Brooklyn, The Continentals that featured the dual lead of Daniel Hicks and Herman Montgomery. Robinson liked both The Channels' "Gleam In Your Eye" and The Continentals' "Dear Lord" /"Fine,Fine Frame".He later recorded "The Closer You Are" as the first Whirlin Disc release.The Continentals went on to make one more record,"Picture Of You"/"Soft and Sweet" before fading into obscurity. The Channels did four sides for Whirlin Disc, gaining popularity,respect and prestige but not much else. After hitting with "That's My Desire" (Gone) and "Altar Of Love" in 1957, The Channels returned to Bobby Robinson, this time for the Fury ("My Love Will Never Die") and Fire labels. At this time, John Felix was intermittently replacing Clifton Wright.On "The Girl Next Door"(Fire),Billy Montgomery and Alton (last name unknown) from The Cellos sang with The Channels.In the early sixties, Larry Hamptden started his own Channells with a mixed men's-women's group for Robinson on Enjoy ("Sad Song").In 1973, The Channels are still going strong with Earl Lewis, John Felix(baritone-bass),Henry Fernandez(first tenor)and Jack Brown(second tenor). What has been most encouraging about this group of revived Channels is that they have produced their own records ("We Belong Together" and "Crazy Mixed Up World") on their own label, Channel.The Channels have been one of the few fifties groups to profit from the naive mistakes of the past.[9]

With the imprint of The Channels,The Charts,Harptones, Willows and Ladders on their minds,five young kids decided, just as everyone else had,to form a group in 1957.From 118th Street,came Ernest "Mickey" Gordy(first tenor), Earl"E.J." Marcus(second tenor),John Marcus(baritone)and Bobby Jeffers (bass).The lead singer,Dave "Pinky" Coleman came from 114th Street.While M.C.'ing an oldies show at The Apollo in 1972, Bobby Jay (Bobby Jeffers) cracked that these guys who became The Laddins were so poor that they had to borrow used uniforms from Anthony and The Imperials. Now it is true that The Laddins shared a storefront with The Imperials on 119th Street and St.Nicholas Avenue,[10] but what certainly has to be true is the poverty of the facilities employed by the Central label to record The Laddins."Did It" was a good New York group sound except that its technical quality added to the "garage" myth hovering over many fifties records. The Laddins may have been singing in a garage or basement but the recording equipment left more to be desired.The record sounded as if it had been recorded on a portable tape recorder. Several years passed until The Laddins decided to sell the master of "Did It" to Irving "Slim" Rose of Times Square Records for $50.00. "Slim" capitalized on the oldies craze of the early sixties, placed "Did It" on his Times Square label and sold it like hot cakes to group sound addicts who frequented his subterranean record shops. Another mistake by a young and carefree fifties group!

In the Spring of 1958, The Laddins recorded "Yes, Oh Baby Yes" with Bobby Jay bassing away for Grey Cliff, a label reportedly owned by Alan Freed and Jack Hook.[11] This turned out to be The Laddins' only hit record as they recorded many others that never did anything including "My Baby's Gone" (unreleased Central), "She's The One" (Aisle), "I Hate To Go Home" (Theatre), "Jump, Shake, Cook and Move"(Bardell) and "Dream Baby" (Butane). The Laddins then did an album in Japan for RCA and masqueraded as The Jarmels and The Paradons before they became The Steinways led by Yvonne Garring in 1966.[12]

The 115th Street area was such a fertile nesting place for vocal groups in the mid-fifties, that it is not actually known how many there were that blossomed forth from this neighborhood. There were others about whom very little is known who sang on or near 115th Street. The collectors' favorite, The Keynotes, emerged from 115th Street in 1954. Although it is rumored that they were singing the street song "Lily Maebelle", their first record for Apollo was "Zenda"/ "Suddenly". Later in 1955, they had a local New York rocker, "I Don't Know" that hit on the R&B stations. It featured Sam "The Man" Taylor on tenor horn and Mickey "Guitar" Baker. The first two records were led by Floyd Adams, who was rumored to be the lead of another Apollo group, The Inspirations ("Raindrops"/"Maggie"). Adams stayed on to do two more groovie rockers "Bye Bye Baby"and"Really Wish You Were Here" until he was replaced by the more dynamic tenor, Sam Kearney, who led "In The Evening" and two different versions of the calypso-blues-rock "Now I Know". The only other known member of The Keynotes was Bernard Matthews. All of the others have remained in obscurity except for first names:"Spanky", "J.D.", Howard, Roger, Lawrence, Randy, and Tucker. The Keynotes were the prototype New York Street group. They may have had as many as ten members who recorded for the fun of it, singing well but never making it big. They were subjected to the same tragic results, limited success and non-recognition as their uptown brothers, The Vocaltones. It is known that one of The Keynotes joined another group from the neighborhood, The Matadors ("Vengeance"-Sue). Two other Matadors were nicknamed

103

"Red" and "Slickback".A third Apollo group,The Cellos,were
known for their jump novelty tunes,"The Japanese (Rang Tang
Ding Dong) Sandman" and "The Juicy Crocodile".But they could
sing beautifully as witnessed by"You Took My Love"and"Under
Your Spell".Alvin Campbell,Billy Montgomery and Alton,were
some of the members of The Cellos.

Another 115th Street group, The Emanons flaunted their
obscurity by their own name-Emanon spelled backwards is "no
name".Robert Colemen(lead),Carl White(second lead and first
tenor),Ralph Steeley(second tenor), James Dukes(baritone)
and James Hill(bass)recorded "Blue Moon" for Josie.[13]

Then there were the Cooper Junior High groups (Madison
Avenue between 119th and 120th Streets).The Desires led by
Frankie Lymon sounding Thomas "Bootsie" White[14] made two
records "Let It Please Be You" and "Rendezvous With You"
for Hull Records in the late fifties.They were reputed to
have also recorded "Mommy And Daddy" as The Students. The
most famous group to come out of the Cooper Talent shows,
The Schoolboys also met the most tragedy.Outside of The Cubs
on Savoy, the originators of the teenaged high tenor leads
were not The Teenagers or The Teenchords but The Schoolboys.
Harold Atley(lead), James (Holland) Edwards(first tenor),
Roger Hayes(second tenor),James "Charlie" McKay(baritone)
and Renaldo Gamble(bass),began at a talent show in Cooper.
Leslie Martin later replaced Atley before the group known
then as The Scobians won first prize on a Ted Mack Original
Amateur Hour.Disc jockey Tommy Smalls renamed them The Schoolboys and in the Fall of 1955,they went on to create the first
nationally successful adolescent tenor record "Please Say
You Want Me"(Okeh).They were managed by James Dailey who
also managed The Desires,Bobbettes[15] and The Demens (Teenage).Somehow The Schoolboys just could not maintain their
early success and totally disintegrated by 1957.[16] Renaldo
Gamble went on to join Pearl McKinnon and The Kodoks("Teenager's Dream", "Oh Gee, Oh Gosh"-Fury). Roger Hayes joined
The Collegians ("Zoom,Zoom, Zoom"-Winley).

James McKay's brother,Lennie McKay,was the lead singer
of a versatile group from 119th Street and Park Avenue,The
Jesters. McKay and Adam Jackson shared leads on soulful bal-
lads "Please Let Me Love You" and "So Strange"-Winley).They
also covered "The Plea" (Chantels)and "The Wind" (Diablos).
All of these records featured the walking blues piano of David
"Baby Cortez" Clowney, a former member of The Pearls and
Valentines.A good uptempo tune, "I Laughed" was recorded

for Paul Winley's subsidiary label,<u>Cyclone</u> in 1959.The Jesters most memorable contributions to the R&B world were the two albums on which they were featured in a battle of the groups with The Paragons,"War" (<u>Winley</u>) and "The Paragons Meet The Jesters" (<u>Jubilee</u>). Other members of The Jesters included Jimmy Smith, Melvin Lewis and Donald Lewis.

With the exception of The Drifters(the Thomas-King group), the groups from the 115th Street area never really became big national stars.They were known locally and some became well established throughout the eastern seaboard's network of theatres and clubs.Their kingdom was the corner,the hallway,the schoolyard and the community center.When they flourished, their home was the kingdom of Rhythm and Blues.

[1]Interview with Ray Pollard,September 11,1971.

[2]Disc jockeys referred to "Do You Love Me" as the "Ajax Cleanser" song because of bass Freddie Donovan's rumbling bass riffs.

[3]Interviews with Richie Davis,Joe and Ralph Martin,January 16,1972.
Interview with Richie Davis,March 5,1972.
Tony Middleton interviewed by Marcia Vance, March 1972.

[4]The complete Willows' discography appears in Bim Bam Boom,Vol.I,Number 6,July 1972,Page 16.

[5]Interview with Ernest Harriston,September 25,1971.

[6]Ernest Harriston interviewed by Steve Flam, September 25, 1971.

[7]Names and information obtained from Kenneth Hamilton, June 1971.

[8]Interview with Leroy Binns and Steven Brown,April 16,1972.

[9]Interview with Earl Lewis,November 27,1971.

[10]Binns and Brown.

[11]Teddy Vann,a member of The Five Cats produced "Yes,Oh Baby Yes".

[12]Interview with Bobby Jay,September 18,1971.

[13]Brown and Hamilton.

[14]The Desires included "Bootsie",Charles Hurston, Charles Powell,George Smith and James Whittier. Jay.

[15]The Bobbettes' hit record,"Mister Lee" was written about the girls' favorite teacher at Cooper Junior High School.

[16]Interview with Edwina Odom,February 1973.

Chapter 7

Sugar Hill

Overlooking the most northern section of Harlem where The
Polo Grounds used to be, is a section baseball diehards used
to refer to as Coogan's Bluff. It stretches from approximately 145th Street to 170th Street and from Edgecombe Avenue
overlooking High Bridge Park on the East to Broadway. Located
there were many parks, schoolyards, bars, and dance halls
where young groups could make themselves heard. To the city
fathers, the neighborhood is known as Washington Heights.
To the street singers of the mid-1950's, this turf was called
Sugar Hill. It would have been nothing for example, for The
Polo Grounds' groups (The Concords or some members of The
Mellomoods and Solitaires) to climb the mountain of stairs
behind The Polo Grounds and go up to St. Nicholas Avenue or
Amsterdam Avenue to challenge one of the early Sugar Hill
groups (The Velvets or The Savoys). Groups from neighborhoods all over Manhattan would cross each other's boundaries
to enter battles of song. The Willows were one group to walk
up to The Hill from 115th Street:

> We used to go and visit the groups in the 150th
> Street area. The whole area was like one small
> neighborhood. Groups were, in a way, parts of
> families. Everybody would go and see the other
> guys perform. Even though it was six or eight
> miles away, we would visit one another. We would
> walk up there and walk back, just singing all
> the way. Never take the subway. If we did take
> the subway, it would be for the echo chamber.[1]

The Velvets were probably the first to make it from Sugar
Hill just as their <u>Red Robin</u> recording brothers, The Vocaleers were the first to make it downtown around 142nd Street
and Amsterdam Avenue. The Velvets included lead singer Charles
Sampson, George Thorpe, Donald Razor, Joe Razor and Bearle
Ashton. They were a highly regarded group receiving three
to four hours of Bobby Robinson's attention when they recorded
their last record "Tell Her"/"I Cried", while an upstart
group, The Scarlets (The Five Satins) were given a matter
of fifteen minutes on the same session.[2] The Velvets made

one early smash that pleaded "I" over and over for Red Robin which followed their first local New York City hit, "They Tried". Before drifting back to total obscurity in 1958, Donald Razor and Leon Briggs recorded "Dance Honey Dance" as The Velvets on Fury 1012. The three Briggs brothers were always in and out of groups on The Hill. Jake Briggs organized a modern harmony group called The Valtones that recorded for Gee. Leon Briggs and Donald Razor were in another Gee group called Johnny Blake and The Clippers.

One Sugar Hill singer who suffered through alternating periods of frustration and commercial success was a young Jimmy Jones. Jones hung out on many corners of The Hill until he entered the service where he met Andrew Barksdale, the bass lead singer of The Berliners, a group that later became The Sparks of Rhythm. Of The Sparks' three recordings for Apollo, their last "Handy Man" was to cause quite a stir in the Rock 'n' Roll world six years later when tenor Jimmy Jones recorded it by himself for Cub Records. While The Sparks of Rhythm were toiling for Apollo, Bobby Moore was returning home from military service in Korea on board ship with Lloyd Price and "Buddy" Bailey (Clovers). Bailey and Moore organized a group on ship that sang many of The Clovers' early fifties recordings; "Fool, Fool, Fool", "One Mint Julep", "Don't You Know I Love You" and "Skylark". When he got back to his old neighborhood which was just below The Hill, Moore quickly became involved in the neighborhood passion for street corner singing. Moore who was from 147th Street and Amsterdam met Jimmy Jones and three other dudes who all came from the 140's and The Amsterdam-Convent Avenue area. This was 1955 when the heyday of the neighborhood Vocaleers had come to an end. Herman Dunham was singing with The Solitaires. Joe Duncan was looking for a new group as "Red" Walker and Melvin Walton left The Vocaleers to join Jones and Moore. In early 1955, Cliff Martinez, a local agent, took the guys to Herman Lubinsky's Savoy Records in Newark. The pattern of naming groups after labels was followed as Jimmy Jones (lead), William Walker (first tenor), Bobby Moore (second tenor), Melvin Walton (baritone) and Kerry Saxton (bass) became known as The Savoys. Their only recording "Say You're Mine" which was later spiced up with electric bass and re-titled "Please Say You're Mine" was a doo-wop fast record with one of the catchiest vocal figures of the period; "doo-wop-wah, doom-wop, wah-sciddle-de-diddle doo" or something like that. In 1956, the quintet found themselves at Rama Records where their name was changed to The Pretenders to cash in on the popular craze for The Platters' "The Great Pretender". It was at this time that the group appeared on two colossal Goldner sponsored stage shows at The Brooklyn Fox and the 125th Street Apollo with The Valentines, Harptones, Joytones, Teenagers, Cleftones and Eddie Cooley and The Dimples. When The Pretenders appeared at these live shows, Lee Gail took the place of Kerry Saxton as bass. Also in 1956, a master of "Close Your Eyes", different than The Five Keys' song, was released on Whirlin Disc and then probably The Pretenders' baddest jam of all, "I Love You So" / "Tonight" was released by Holiday in 1958. The group had one more record as The Pretenders for Apt ("Blue And Lonely") before they changed their name to Jimmy Jones and The Jones Boys ("Heaven In Your Eyes" - Arrow). The group then broke up with Gail and Moore joining The Vocaltones. In 1960, Jones went out on his own, working at a luncheonette on 147th and Amsterdam to save enough money to later smash the charts with "Handy Man" and "Good Timin'".[3]

There were other groups who sang on The Hill or in the surrounding area. Gaining brief recognition were Butchie Saunders and The Elchords, Eddie "Puddin'" Carson and The Royaltones, Richard Brown and The Ebonaires, The Rocketones of "Mexico" fame and The Collegians (Vernon Riley, Roger Hayes, Henry Brown, William Tarkenton, and Holland Jackson) but The Sugar Hill groups that really made an impact on the world of Rhythm and Blues and Rock 'n' Roll were The Valentines and The Teenagers.

In 1972, Jimmy Castor, singer, composer, arranger, alto and tenor saxophonist extraordinaire remarked that he grew up with, sang with, and wrote for the first super R&B vocal group. Frankie Lymon, Sherman Garnes, Herman Santiago, Jimmy Merchant and Joe Negroni met in the schools and on the streets of Sugar Hill before they became known as The Teenagers. The Teenagers, like so many other adolescent street singers, began imitating and emulating the older R&B group acts who had scored with hit records. The result for The Cubs, The Schoolboys, Teenagers, Hemlocks, Young Lads, Teenchords, Tellers and many others was not the true soulful R&B sound of the early fifties; but the young adolescent high tenor lead sound of 1956. The national successes of The Schoolboys and Teenagers started a chain reaction of school age adolescent boy-soprano groups. The Uniqueteens, Richard Lanham and The Tempotones of Philadelphia and The Chanters were some more who succeeded. On Sugar Hill, The Teenagers had started a trend while in fact they themselves were the result of the trend of emulating the older guys.

In 1954, The Angels, a group from Philadelphia (25th and

Diamond Streets) won two amateur night contests at The Apollo. The group never recorded and returned to its neighborhood, the borderline between The Mohawks and The Village Gangs where The Buccaneers (Southern and Rama) had originated. The Angels' impoverished lead singer, Richard Barrett, then left Philadelphia to come to New York City to make his fame and fortune. The "Big Apple", however, had other ideas. A destitute Barrett wandered around Washington Heights, playing his ukulele until he bumped into four cats chirping very loudly on the corner of 157th Street and Amsterdam Avenue. He told The Dreamers who were Ray "Pops" Briggs, Ronnie Bright, Carl Hogan and Mickey Francis (lead) that he had written a song. The Dreamers who sang at parties and community centers were trying to make it on their own and wanted no part of someone else's song.

Later in 1954, The Dreamers performed their first gig at Bowman's on 155th Street and St. Nicholas Place (the heart of Sugar Hill). Barrett went into the club, played the song on his ukulele, The Dreamers huddled and then surprisingly he was asked to sing it with them. The Dreamers had difficulty on their first few gigs:

We sang (at Bowman's), two of the twelve people in the bar clapped and we were paid exactly one dollar each. Before we became professionals, if you really want to call it that, we did most of our singing around junior high schools (J.H.S.135) in a battle of the groups type thing. We also appeared...at The Englewood(New Jersey)Jewish Center where we battled The Harptones. We killed them on the first show with our three dollar coats and they came back on the second show and murdered us. It was a hell of a thing. On another occasion in 1954, we entered amateur night at The Apollo and won third place. We were beaten out by, of all things, a belly dancer, a shake dancer. We were supposed to wear jackets but "Pops" had taken his jacket and put it in a washing machine; a dress jacket mind you. He came to the theatre in a rough dried coat. To solve the problem, we took our coats off and went out in our shirt sleeves (to sing "Money Honey"). 4

The Dreamers who began by digging The Vocaleers at a local Friday night "grind 'em up" in the Colonial Projects next to The Polo Grounds, had to take in Richard Barrett as lead singer to add the original song, "Tonight Kathleen" to their repertoire. At this time, Carl Hogan had a disagreement with the group and left. Donald Razor from the old Velvets replaced him. The group went to Hy Weiss' Old Town Records office in the cloak room of the old Triboro Theatre on 125th Street and Third Avenue to audition with "Tonight Kathleen". The name Valentines was chosen in the usual way from all the categories of flowers, birds and names referring to love and lovers. Richard Barrett (lead), Mickey Francis (first tenor), Donald Razor (second tenor), Ray "Pops" Briggs (baritone) and Ronnie Bright (bass), recorded "Tonight Kathleen" and "Summer Love" for Old Town with negligible results. About a year passed until Barrett brought the street song "Lily Maebelle" to George Goldner. There are many rumors that exist about the origin of this song with the bass and harmony beginning, the provocative lead, chattering background harmony, blaring saxophone of Jimmy Wright and fade away ending. It was rumored that "Lily Maebelle" was sung in the streets by either The Keynotes or Donald Razor and The Velvets. Another story had The Valentines rehearsing at Ray Briggs' house where his sister was cooking in the kitchen. They asked her to suggest a title for a song. That is supposedly how "Lily Maebelle" came about. After the release of the song, the emergence of The Valentines as a forceful group came when they were signed to appear at The State Theatre in Hartford with Alan Freed. Barrett, who had taken months to find a job in New York, was at first reluctant to go off on a singing odyssey. His skepticism, however, was confirmed while working on a landscaping job that year. While he was working, "Lily Maebelle" was played on the radio. He told his co-workers, "Hey, that's my record, that's me singing". The response was "get outta here".[5] Richard had just been too poor for too long for a record being played on the radio to have any impact.

The Valentines developed quite a reputation while gigging at the Freed and Tommy Smalls' shows and battling against The Opals and The Cadillacs at Rockland Palace. There was never much money involved for the groups at these neighborhood gigs. The one group that bested the others could bask in the sunshine of prestige and recognition and walk down the street holding their heads high as peacocks. The bad rap against The Valentines was that they could not sing well. On their early Rama ballads, "Falling For You", "Hand Me Down Love", "Christmas Prayer", "Why", and "Twenty Minutes", there was just a lot of ooh-wahing. The fast songs such as "The Woo Woo Train" and "I Love You Darling" were true doo-wop records. In fact,the latter was a page right out of The Crows' song book. The Valentines had a habit of not sounding too well in person. But they could dance! Decked out in their heart adorned white suits with red shirts,pink bow ties and black patent leather shoes, The Valentines would come out on stage in a line representing a locomotive in "The Woo Woo Train". They had fancy steps and each could dance well by himself.They had taught themselves their own choreography without hiring the services of an instructor.

The Valentines continued to make two more recordings for Rama. These were their most beautiful and best performed ballads;"Nature's Creation" and "Don't Say Goodnight".Just prior to the recording of "Nature's Creation",Dave "Baby" Cortez replaced "Pops" Briggs.Previously,Eddie Edghill had replaced Donald Razor before the switch from Old Town to Rama. Finally on their last record,Carl Hogan rejoined to replace Eddie Edghill after leaving his Sugar Hill group,The Miracles, to sing lead on "Don't Say Goodnight".[6]

It was during this period of The Valentines that Barrett and Cortez began to get involved in audio, repertoire and head arrangement work.Many of the neighborhood youngsters knew about this as they began to seek out their idols,particularly Barrett.One night in 1955,The Teenagers started singing under Barrett's window on 161st Street to get his attention.Barrett was not really interested in putting in a full day at The Apollo to return home to listen to four kids under his window accompany some Spanish sounding kid on "Lily Maebelle". Gradually, Barrett was attracted to the idea of a Rhythm and Blues song being sung with a Spanish accent; but every time he went downstairs,they would run away.Finally,one day,he promised to listen to them,if they would only stop camping underneath his window.He set up a 7 P.M. appointment for an audition on the following Monday at Stitt Junior High School, the school the boys attended. Barrett forgot about the appointment until 7 P.M. that Monday. He rushed uptown to find the five kids still anxiously waiting for him.They sang some of The Valentines' songs.The harmony was good.Tall Sherman had an amazingly low voice for such a young kid.Frankie was ooh-wahing as second tenor and Herman Santiago was singing lead."Do you have any songs?"asked Richard.They sang a poem some lady had written called "Why Do Fools Fall In Love". Richard made a few alterations in the song to fit into the only four chords he could play on the piano.On the day The Teenagers were to audition for George Goldner, Herman caught a bad cold. The fate of the hunter prevailed as no one else in the group knew the lyrics except Frankie. He started singing the song and Richard loved it. At the time, Goldner had a group called The Millionaires (managed by Lover Patterson) who were really Ben E. King and some of The Five Crowns. Barrett threatened that if Goldner did not record the group with the little kid who had the twinkle in his eye, he would not rehearse Goldner's Millionaires. Goldner agreed to let the kids record two songs during The Millionaires' dinner break. The Millionaires went on to become a piece of Rock 'n' Roll trivia until they emerged as Ben E. King and The Drifters. The Teenagers went on to become millionaires or at least people believed that to be true.

Here growing up on the streets of Sugar Hill (Edgecombe Avenue and 165th Street) was a little boy who lit up like a Christmas tree every time he approached a microphone. A little boy who went as far as his imagination could carry him and all because of "The Woo Woo Train" and "Lily Maebelle". Frankie Lymon soon became a giant in the neighborhood but there were always the doubtful skeptics and tough kids who just could not believe that a little ninth grader was a Rock'n'Roll star. Jimmy Castor whose group The Juniors, Al Casey (bass), Orton Graves (baritone) and Johnny Williams (tenor) had earlier recorded one of Lymon's million sellers, "Promise To Remember", remarked that people in the neighborhood regarded Frankie as a monster but that there were also the cynics; "You made a record? Ah, that ain't nothin'". [7]

As natural a born talent as he was, Lymon was in a way a vocal reincarnation of Barrett. Barrett taught Lymon a certain style of singing. Barrett was able to inject into Lymon what he wanted to do himself but was not able to do. Many of the phrasings in The Teenagers' hit records were copies of the vocalizing on "Tonight Kathleen" and "Lily Maebelle". Lymon had an uncanny ability to take what Barrett taught and glorify it. He would take choreography and do it much better than Barrett could ever teach him. Lymon was a solid natural. A true born star at the age of thirteen with all the "presence" and poise of a stage veteran. He would come out on stage and set the whole world on fire.

Another star who reflected Barrett's lessons was Arlene Smith, the lead voice of The Chantels. There are two stories about how this teenaged group of girls managed to meet their mentor. There is the version that the girls hung around outside an Alan Freed show at The Brooklyn Paramount until Richard and "Baby" Cortez would listen to them. The other is that Arlene, Sonia Goring, Rene Minus, Jackie Landry and Lois Harris were heard singing in a rehearsal hall at 53rd Street and Broadway over the marquee where "Mr. Wonderful" was playing in 1957. Allegedly someone had promised to teach the girls how to sing, if they would pay him three dollars apiece. Barrett thought that was outrageous as the girls sounded like a church choir. He asked them to sing again outside under the marquee. He was astounded and wondered how a choir would sound singing a Rhythm and Blues tune. He recorded "The Plea" and "Maybe", two of Arlene's songs with The Chantels. While this two sided hit was selling very quietly, Barrett and his friend Bobby Spencer (Cadillacs) wrote two songs for The Teenagers in his old bedroom on 161st Street. Spencer sold his song outright for $50.00 while Barrett peddled his for an advance of $150.00 and writer's royalties. What were the two songs? Two that were probably the most appropriate ever recorded by Frankie Lymon and The Teenagers; "I'm Not A Juvenile Delinquent" and "The ABC's Of Love" respectively. Then Arlene Smith wrote a song called "Maybe" that Richard arranged on his piano in the only way he knew with those little triplets he played. The piano beginning was his signature on just about every hit record on the Gone and End labels. "Maybe" went over the top and was a second big smash for him. Then came Little Anthony and The Imperials. There was a music publisher, Al Lewis with whom Richard did not get along. The man had given Richard a demo by Bobby Darin of a song that was a groove. Richard would play the song one morning and throw it out the next. Meanwhile, Anthony Guordine had a habit of talking like a little kid. Eureka! It would be perfect for Anthony to chop up the words while Richard accompanied with his four piano chords. The result? "Tears On My Pillow"- a million seller. The same formula was continued on "Oh Yeah", "So Much", "Wishful Thinking", and "When You Wish Upon A Star".

Barrett continued producing for The Isley Brothers, The Flamingos (The "Flamingo Serenade" LP) and The Dubs. Then he sang lead with Jackie, Rene and Sonia on "Summer's Love" and later united the three with Annette Smith, the former lead of The Veneers for Carlton Records. "Look In My Eyes" and "Well I Told You" (the answer to "Hit The Road Jack") were two more hit records. In 1960, Barrett went out on his own again thinking he was Billy Eckstine with "Smoke Gets In Your Eyes" (MGM). Then he met some cats jammin' around 125th Street and Lenox Avenue, called The Sevilles and recorded "Dream On"/ "I Am Yours" (Seville). In 1964, he produced Harold Melvin and The Blue Notes' "Get Out" with John

114

Atkins singing lead (<u>Landa</u>). Later came The Red Caps, The Three Degrees ("Gee Baby I'm Sorry") and Norman Johnson and The Showmen. The latter today are R&B chart busters known as General Johnson and The Chairman of The Board.[8]

Today Barrett is a producer with Gamble-Huff and the director, manager, creator of the dynamic Three Degrees. Quite a step up for the landscape gardener from Sugar Hill. His real gift to the music world, the little man with the lovable voice and twinkle in his eye, had died aimlessly in February, 1968, at the tender age of only 28. Frankie Lymon made one last record "I'm Sorry"/"Sea Breeze". His voice had changed but it still had the same old vibrato. But what is really eerie is that he sounded so much the way his old pal Jimmy Castor sounds today. Who knows what might have been?

<u>They</u> <u>All</u> <u>Sang</u> <u>On</u> <u>The</u> <u>Corner</u> has been limited mostly to the street corners of New York City. Time, space and finances have prevented ample treatment of all of the Rhythm and Blues vocal groups who originally sang on the corners of American cities in the forties, fifties and early sixties. In depth accounts of many important groups such as The Flamingos, The Dell-Vikings, Clovers, Spaniels, Penguins, Coasters, The Five Satins, Nutmegs, Hollywood Flames, The Platters, and countless others have been omitted for the sake of brevity or the lack of complete and accurate information. It is hoped that this book is only a beginning and that others will explore the contributions to our culture made by other artists of street corner singing.

[1] Interview with Tony Middleton, April 8, 1972.

[2] Interview with Fred Parris, July 9, 1971.

[3] Interview with Bobby Moore, February 11, 1973.

[4] Interview with Carl Hogan, January 30, 1972.

[5] Interview with Richard Barrett, April 30, 1972.

[6] During his hiatus from The Valentines, Carl Hogan formed a group called The Miracles (Hogan, Leon Briggs, Jerry Moore, Lee Gail and Joe Razor). They recorded "Your Love"/"I Love You So" (Fury 1001). Earlier Hogan sang in a Robert and Johnny type duo with Charles Sampson, the former lead of The Velvets. Charles and Carl recorded "Lucky Star"/ "One More Chance" (Red Robin 137). When he rejoined The Valentines, Hogan teamed with Barrett writing "Don't Say Goodnight", "Be Sure My Love" (Dubs), "So Much" (Little Anthony and The Imperials) and "Is It True" (Mickey and Sylvia). Today Carl Hogan is an accomplished composer-arranger of contemporary material.

[7] Interview with Jimmy Castor, August 18, 1972.

[8] Barrett.

ACKNOWLEDGEMENTS

Thanks to those who helped and were included or not included in this book.

J.R.Bailey
Hank Ballard
Fred Barksdale
Eddie Barnes
Reggie Barnes
Clarence Bassett
Bobby Baylor
Jimmy Beckum
Leroy Binns
Ron Blackman
William Blakely
Richard Blandon
Lil Briggs
Ronnie Bright
Steven Brown
Zeke Carey
Earl Carroll
Jimmy Castor
Linda Champion
"Big" Bob Czartoryski
Curtis Cherebin
Raoul Cita
Richie Davis
Billy Dawn
Abel DeCosta
William Dempsey
Arnold Dodge
Cleve Duncan
Barbara Edwards
Steve Flam
Richard Freeman
Mr.& Mrs.R.Galgano
William Galloway
Carl Gardner
Gus Gossert
James Griffin
Anthony Gourdine
Ken Hamilton
Rita Haracz
Ernest Harriston
Carl Hogan
Dick Horlick

Henry Jackson
Ernie Kaschauer
Earl Lewis
Milton Love
Dr.Warren Lowey
Harold Lucas
Linda Lynch
Leroy MacNiel
Clyde McPhatter
Larry Marshak
Joe Martin
Ralph Martin
Roland Martinez
Tony Middleton
Sal Mondrone
Bobby Moore
Barbara Murray
Lowe Murray
Ralph Newman
Lawrence O'Boyle
Edwina Odom
Fred Parris
Gene Pearson
Ray Pollard
Jimmy Ricks
Vernon Riley
Bobby Schiffman
Frank Schiffman
James Shea
Arlene Smith
Bobby Spencer
Sam Strain
Nolan Strong
Warren Suttles
Mr.& Mrs.Fred Taylor
Sonny Til
Bobby Thomas
Hy Weiss
Rudy West
Buzzy Willis
Mr.& Mrs.Willie Winfield
Paul Winley

The Rivileers: (l-r) Gene Pearson, Milton Edwards, Alfonso Delaney, Mel Dancey and Herb Crosby.
Photo by Maurice Seymour

The Swallows After "Junior" Denby: (l-r) "Money" Johnson, Earl Hurley, Eddie Rich, Dee Ernie Bailey and Irving Turner. Bailey and Turner had replaced original members, Norris "Bunky" Mack and Denby, respectively. (Photo-courtesy of Willie Winfield)

119.

The Four Fellows with David Jones on lead. (Photo by Charles Stewart).

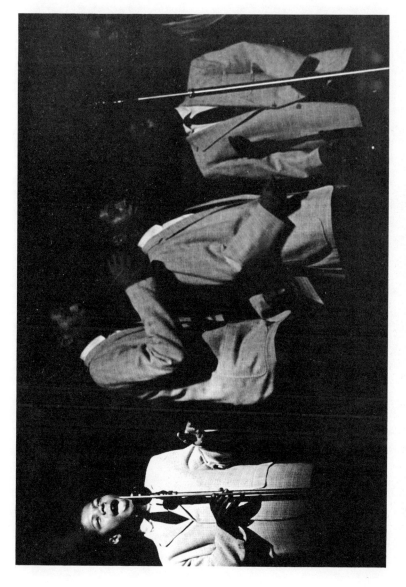

Immortals All - The Teenagers: (l-r) Frankie Lymon, Sherman Garnes, Joe Negroni, Herman Santiago and Jimmy Merchant. (Photo by Charles Stewart).

The Five Royales Featuring Lowman Pauling. (Photo by Charles Stewart).

Guess Who? (l-r) Jimmy Bailey, Earl Wade, Charles Brooks, Earl Carroll, Bobby Phillips, chauffeur Rudy Bailey and band eader, Jesse Powell. (Photo by Charles Stewart).

"Fine Little Girl": Raoul Cita accompanying The Harptones at the Piano. (Photo by Charles Stewart).

The Harptones at The Apollo in 1956: (l-r) William Dempsey, Jimmy Beckum, Billy Brown and Willie Winfield. (Photo by Charles Stewart).

The Apollo Marquee in 1956. (Photo by Charles Stewart).

The Fabulous Flamingos: (l-r) Zeke Carey, Jake Carey, Paul Wilson, Johnny Carter and Nate Nelson. (Photo by Charles Stewart).

"South of The Border" - The Solitaires: (l-r) Buzzy Willis, Pat Gaston, Milton Love, Bobby Baylor and Monte Owens. (Photo by Charles Stewart).

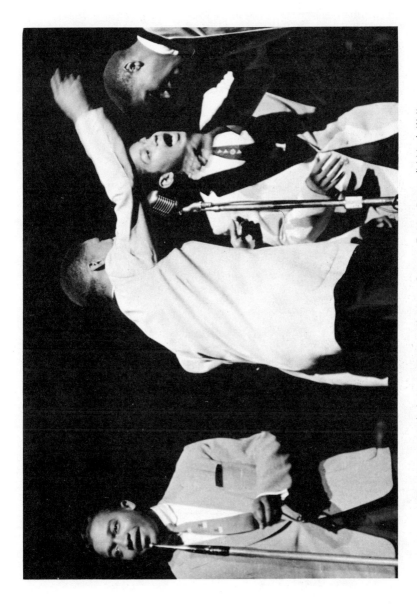

The Heartbeats: (l-r) James Sheppard, Albert Crump, Robby Brown (hidden), Wally Roker and Vernon Seavers. (Photo by Charles Stewart).

The Valentines Demonstrate Their Choreography: (bottom l-r) Richard Barrett, Mickey Francis, Ron Bright, Ray Briggs and Eddie Edghill. (Photo by Charles Stewart). These three picutres are a sequence of their show.

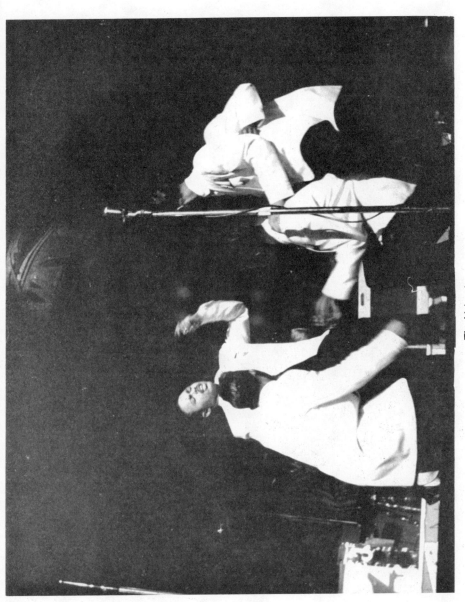

The Valentines

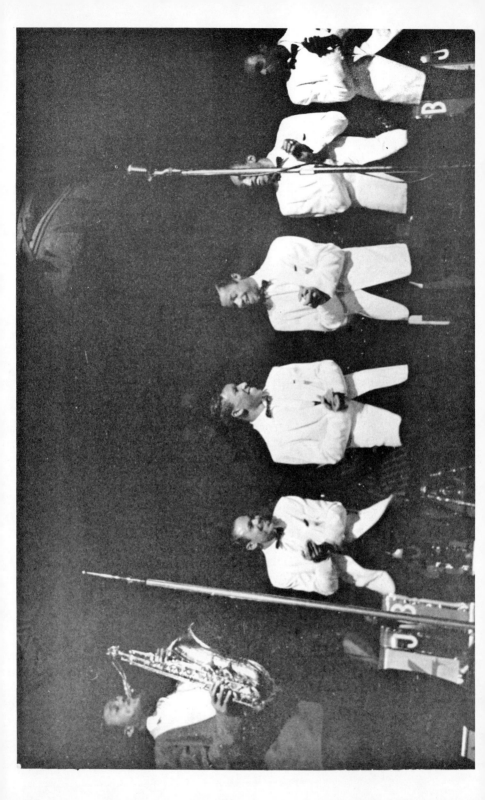

The Late Tommy "Dr. Jive" Smalls. (Photo by Charles Stewart)

The late Alan Freed. (Photo by Charles Stewart).

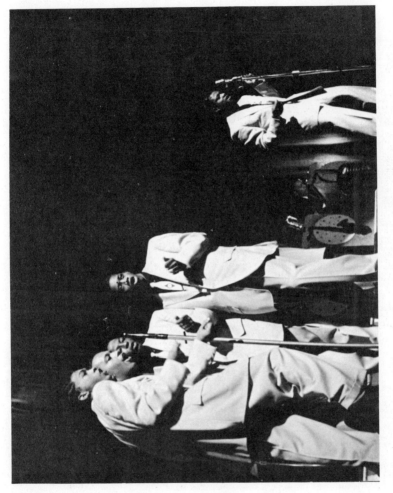

Otis Williams and the Charms who covered many artists including The Five Keys ("Ling Ting Tong") and The Jewels ("Hearts of Stone"). (Photo by Charles Stewart.)

"Heidi, Heidi, Ho . . . You Gonna Make Me Lose My Mind" - The Nutmegs at the Uptown: (l-r) James Griffin, James Tyson, Leory Griffin, Leroy MacNiel and Billy Emery. (Photo by Charles Stewart.)

136.

The Willows: (l-r) Tony Middleton, Joe Martin, Ralph Martin, John Thomas Steele and Richie Davis. (Photo by James Kriegsmann.)

137.

The Pretenders: Jimmy Jones, (bottom l-r) Lee Gail, William Walker, Bobby Moore and Melvin Walton. (Photo by Glamor Pix).

The Penguins: Dexter Tisby, Curtis Williams, Bruce Tate and (in front) Cleveland Duncan. (Photo donated by Frank Schiffman.)

The Original Moonglows and Moonlighters: (l-r) Harvey Fuqua, Bobby Lester, Prentiss Barnes, "Pete" Graves and guitarist, Billy Johnson. (Photo by James Kriegsmann).

Three of the Cardinals sing at the Uptown: (l-r) Donald "Jack" Johnson (baritone), Meredith "Chinch" Brothers (first tenor) and Ernie Lee Warren (lead). Original Cardinals not shown are Leon "Tree" Hardy (bass) and "Sam" Aydelotte (second tenor - guitarist). Photo by Charles Stewart.

The Diamonds whose cover records of The Gladiolas ("Little Darlin' "), The Solitaires ("Walkin' Along") and The Willows ("Church Bells May Ring") sold millions. (Photo by Charles Stewart).

The Original Orioles: (top Alexander Sharp, George Nelson, Sonny Til, (bottom), Tommy Gaither and Johnny Reed. (Photo-courtesy of Bim Bam Boom magazine.)

The Opals (Crystals): (top) Johnny Hopson, Earl Wade, (bottom) Teddy Williams and Martin Brown. (Photo - courtesy of Dick Horlick.)

The Keynotes featuring Floyd Adams with Howard Anderson (first tenor), Roger Harris (second tenor), Larry "Spanky" Carter (baritone) and Tucker Clark (bass). (Photo by Diaz - courtesy of Dick Horlick.)

The Blenders: (top l-r) Ollie Jones (second tenor), James DeLoach (bass), Abel DeCosta (first tenor), (bottom) Tommy Irving Adams (baritone) and Ernie Brown (guitarist). (Photo by James Kriegsmann.)

The Fi-Tones Quintet in 1958: (top) Ron Anderson, (center) Gene Redd, Cecil Holmes, Lowe Murray and (bottom) Reggie Barnes. (Photo - donated by Willie Winfield). (Photo by Edward A. Bagwell).

INDEX

A resident of New York's upper East Side, Phil Groia has gathered the data in this book over the years. He is Research Coordinator and a Feature Writer for Bim Bam Boom. He also teaches Social Studies in the Stony Brook area of Long Island.

"The Cadillacs were the stage masters of unparalleled choreography....."

"The Skylarks/Harptones became the classic example of the early New York street corner singing groups....."

"Sonny Til and The Orioles, as Jubilee later decided to bill them, were the pioneers of the big stage acts..."

This book contains over 450 references to groups and individuals who made Rhythm and Blues become "big time".